The Research Tool Ki

The Research Tool Kit

PUTTING IT ALL TOGETHER

Bruce D. Friedman

WAYNE STATE UNIVERSITY

Brooks/Cole Publishing Company

I(T)P® An International Thomson Publishing Company

Pacific Grove • Albany • Belmont • Bonn • Boston • Cincinnati • Detroit • Johannesburg • London
Madrid • Melbourne • Mexico City • New York • Paris • Singapore • Tokyo • Toronto • Washington

Sponsoring Editor: *Lisa I. Gebo*
Marketing Team: *Jean Vevers Thompson,*
 Deanne Brown, and Romy Taormina
Editorial Assistants: *Terry Thomas and*
 Shelley Bouhaja
Production Coordinator: *Laurel Jackson*
Production Assistant: *Karen Morgan*

Manuscript Editor: *Patterson Lamb*
Interior Design: *Carolyn Deacy*
Cover Design: *Roy R. Neuhaus*
Cover Illustration: *Jose Ortega*
Art Editors: *Jennifer Mackres and Harry Briggs*
Typesetting: *Susan Rogin*
Printing and Binding: *Patterson Printing*

COPYRIGHT© 1998 by Brooks/Cole Publishing Company
A division of International Thomson Publishing Inc.
I(T)P The ITP logo is a registered trademark under license.

For more information, contact:

BROOKS/COLE PUBLISHING COMPANY
511 Forest Lodge Road
Pacific Grove, CA 93950
USA

International Thomson Editores
Seneca 53
Col. Polanco
11560 México, D. F., México

International Thomson Publishing Europe
Berkshire House 168–173
High Holborn
London WC1V 7AA
England

International Thomson Publishing GmbH
Königswinterer Strasse 418
53227 Bonn
Germany

Thomas Nelson Australia
102 Dodds Street
South Melbourne, 3205
Victoria, Australia

International Thomson Publishing Asia
221 Henderson Road
#05–10 Henderson Building
Singapore 0315

Nelson Canada
1120 Birchmount Road
Scarborough, Ontario
Canada M1K 5G4

International Thomson Publishing Japan
Hirakawacho Kyowa Building, 3F
2-2-1 Hirakawacho
Chiyoda-ku, Tokyo 102
Japan

Printed in the United States of America

10 9 8 7 6 5 4 3 2 1

Library of Congress Cataloging-in-Publication Data
Friedman, Bruce D., [date]
 The research tool kit : putting it all together / Bruce D.
Friedman.
  p. cm.
 Includes bibliographical references.
 ISBN 0–534–34409–7 (alk. paper)
 1. Social service—Research—Methodology. I. Title.
HV11.F75 1998
361.3′2′072—dc21   97–21796
                                     CIP

About the Author

Bruce D. Friedman is an associate professor at Wayne State University, where he is also the coordinator of the bachelor of social work program in the School of Social Work. Dr. Friedman has conducted qualitative research on delivery services for the homeless, based on an ecological systems perspective. He is co-author of *Social Support Networks: A Bibliography, 1983–1987* and sole author of *No Place Like Home: A Study of Two Homeless Shelters.* Dr. Friedman has also published several articles, including "Overcoming Barriers to Homeless Delivery Services: A Community Response."

Contents

Preface

Why do students seem to struggle with research? This was one of the questions that troubled me as an aspiring social work academic. After 15 years of direct social work experience, including being an agency director, I entered a doctoral program and discovered that most of my fellow students seemed almost completely turned off to research. As an agency director, I was constantly faced with issues of accountability of practice. Accountability and justifying one's effectiveness were key elements in maintaining program funding, and making these connections could not be done easily without research results. I returned to academia for the chance to share my knowledge with others and found this general fear about research. I had not intended to become a research teacher, but my experience in bringing measurable steps into practice helped direct me to this path. This book became an outgrowth of my interest in dividing the tasks in the social work process into steps that can be quantified and measured.

That process did not occur overnight. Not until I started my dissertation and taught my own research course did I begin to discover some of the reasons that students had problems with contextual aspects of research. Research was presented in very abstract terms, using large data sets, proving information with sample sizes in the thousands. From a practitioner's perspective, research was unrealistic. As a student with the future aim of helping people, I saw little linkage between working with a single client and conducting research projects with large samples. This led to another question: How do people translate the procedures that contributed to the findings of the large projects to the few clients they will see as part of the field experience? Unless there was a way to translate research to a realistic procedure, the research would be an impractical, obscure component of the curriculum.

Contributing to this dilemma was the status of funded social work research that was heavily focused on quantitative measures. I recall talking to staff members at the National Institute of Mental Health about a homeless shelter study I wanted to do. They told me that, because the study was qualitative, they would not fund it. (Things are changing now, but that was the state of affairs in the 1980s.) Finding agencies that were willing to fund small, qualitative studies was very difficult. I found that many students were not interested in doing large-sample studies because these projects did not relate to their areas of interest. Rather, they wanted to understand the change process with individual clients. Thus, they perceived research as something foreign, something that could be done only with large data sets.

Thanks to discussions with Howard Goldstein, I began to realize that there were two types of people doing research: compilers and creators. I saw that much of the funded research was built on proving existing pieces of knowledge, or compiling. There was plenty of room for people to be creators, but, unless the creators had a way to measure and share the information they were discovering, compilers would continue to gather and analyze existing pieces of information that were just cut differently. People doing individual case study research needed a way to realize the value in the work they were doing and to share it with the world, for the nature of case study research is important in understanding truth. The way to make that possible was to integrate research principles into social work practice methods.

This Tool Kit is my effort to integrate research methods into practice, not only for social work, but for all the social sciences. I call it a Tool Kit because it does not teach research but is to be used in tandem with a research text. This text is a tool, something used to assist in the research process. In addition, because it separates out the parts of the research method, it is not a single tool but a collection of tools that help to make the process manageable. I have used this method with both bachelor's and master's degree students in a classroom setting where I have asked them to apply the text to their field experience to integrate field work and research. They have found this a valuable process. I have also shared the Tool Kit with doctoral candidates struggling with how to proceed with their own research projects. They, too, have found it helpful. I hope that in using the Tool Kit, you have the same experiences that others have had. I present it to you as a way to break the process into steps to assist you in learning and doing research. On completing the Tool Kit, you will have created your own project. I hope you enjoy the process!

Acknowledgments

I would like to thank the reviewers of this book for their valuable insights and suggestions. These reviewers include Sharon K. Collins, Anderson University; Henry J. D'Souza, University of Nebraska; Jonathan C. Finkelstein, University of Maryland Baltimore County; Wayne Lanning, University of Nevada–Las Vegas; George S. Morrison, University of Texas; Mary Swigonski, Rutgers University–Newark Campus; and Barbara Thomlison, University of Calgary.

Bruce D. Friedman

The Research Tool Kit

CHAPTER ONE

What Is Research?

To a student, the term *research* is often scary. It is usually associated with a form of scientific inquiry that relates to the physical sciences. However, research is a part of everything we do. It is a thought process we use to solve problems, a method of inquiry that helps us build knowledge. In essence, research is a scientific process we use in every aspect of our lives. What has made it scary is the association that has evolved around the term. The physical sciences have used the word *research* to relate to big number sets with large statistical probabilities. Many students have admitted that the reason they selected certain majors was to avoid the math associated with these large statistical sets. Some of your experiences in science or mathematics may have been unpleasant, leading you to pursue an educational path in areas where these disciplines are not predominant. In reality, research is a logical thinking process for building knowledge. This Tool Kit will provide you with a workable step-by-step approach to research. It gives you a practical application of logical thought processes to help you integrate your practicum experience into a research project.

Understanding Science

Science is built on two different realities: what is observed and what is agreed on. What we observe is not always what is agreed on. The difference between the two creates a sense of two different types of reality in the world.

These two types of reality lead to two different views of the world. There is the static view, or what is built on facts and knowledge. These facts and knowledge are based on an interrelated set of propositions about particular observations or a particular set of empirical phenomena. Empirical phenomena are observations that have been tested again and again. For example, when we let an object fall from our hands, we are aware that it will drop to the floor. We have given the name *gravity* to the force that causes objects to drop, and we understand how it works after repeated observations of releasing things from our hands and seeing them fall.

Because there is agreement about these observations—acceptance that is based on both logical and empirical support—these observations lead to propositions. Propositions are used to help explain events in nature. When these propositions are recurrent, we can use them to predict what we should be observing. We call these *theories*.

However, what we observe does not always match the anticipated observations. We begin to see a discrepancy between what we observe and what the set of propositions tells us we should observe. This mismatch leads to a dynamic view of science based on process or activity. This process or activity then leads to a need for further observations. We analyze the additional observations to determine whether we can find logical explanations for them. If we can, we then try to discover if the original theory is faulty and we have a new theory. These observations lead to *empirical generalizations*.

As an example, the 1980s saw an increase in the number of homeless people in this country. The early literature placed the problem on a lack of affordable housing and the gentrification of America's cities (Reamer, 1989). The solution was to build more affordable housing. However, when new housing was constructed the problem of homelessness persisted and even expanded. Evidently, additional observations were needed to explain other factors that were contributing to the increase of homeless people (Friedman, 1994). The additional observations identified a number of contributors to the problem. One such factor was barriers to people in marginal circumstances that prevented them from accessing the support systems developed to prevent homelessness. These barriers could be categorized into four groups: (1) "systems" issues that prevent cohesive planning and delivery of services, (2) attitudes held by homeless people toward the service delivery system, (3) attitudes of the workers within those service delivery systems toward homeless people, (4) underlying community values that could maintain a segment of the population as homeless (Friedman & Levine-Holdowsky, 1997). Another factor was the closing of mental institutions without adequate community support, in addition to the lack of affordable housing. The additional observations led to empirical generalizations about the reasons homelessness was increasing. As these empirical observations accumulate, then we can build theory.

The relationship between theories, hypotheses, observations, and empirical generalizations is depicted in Figure 1.1. This cycle demonstrates a scientific process that is interactive, with each step building on the other. The development of science, especially in the social sciences, is a constant ebb and flow wherein repeated observations are used to build empirical generalizations. These lead to

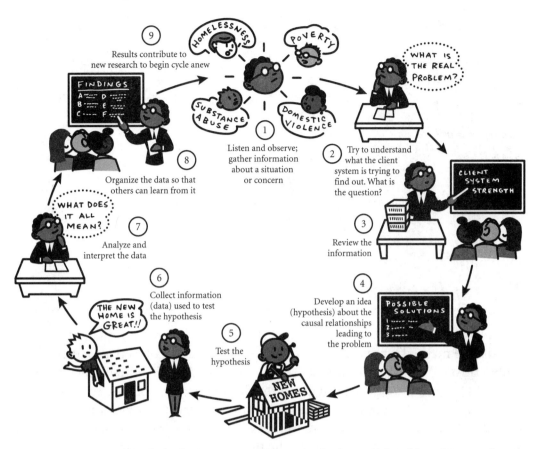

Figure 1.1   The work of social scientists. Social scientists look at social problems/issues and develop solutions in an orderly, systematic manner. They use a problem-solving approach that builds on client system strengths to arrive at solutions. This process is called *research*. The social scientist takes the steps shown here.

theories from which hypotheses are constructed, to be tested by observations. Using the theories to create a probability statement that explains the relationship between certain phenomena is called developing a hypothesis. The whole cycle is called the *inductive/deductive* cycle of theory construction and relates to the struggle between knowing and building knowledge (see Figure 1.2). The inductive side uses observations to build theories that explain events in society. The deductive side uses the theories to draw conclusions that explain how things should work.

For a variety of reasons, the state of the social sciences is not at a point where its theories can explain what happens in society. Because our theories do not consistently explain events, we need continuous observations with which to adapt the theories and thus reach a better understanding and explanation of events in the world. The social sciences are considered young sciences with very few theories that explain phenomena. Instead, they consist of a number of small or midrange theories that explain parts of phenomena. This leads to a struggle between forms of scientific inquiry and is called the quantitative/qualitative research debate.

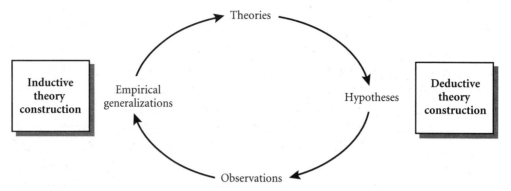

Figure 1.2   The inductive/deductive cycle of theory construction

Types of Research

Research can be divided into two major types: quantitative and qualitative. The quantitative method emphasizes the production of precise, objective, and generalizable statistical findings (Rubin & Babbie, 1997, p. 26). The qualitative method emphasizes depth of understanding and the deeper meaning of human experience that are used with the aim of generating theoretically rich observations (Rubin & Babbie, 1997). The quantitative method is used when the theories dictate the nature of the observation to be made. The theories direct the form of the hypotheses that are then tested.

A *theory* describes an interrelationship between the concepts in a set of concepts. It is the interrelationship that leads to the ability to predict events. Theories then provide clues or suggestions for interventions. We use theories to help explain things we do not understand. Theories can help us organize agreed-on observations or facts about some particular phenomena. A theory has three main functions: to organize, to explain, and to predict. The three functions of theories lead to the development of hypotheses.

Theories help *organize* the information about a particular event. Once the facts of the event are organized, theories can help to *explain* the event. This knowledge is then used to *predict* future occurrences of similar events. For example, think about the theory of gravity. Newton organized the information surrounding all items of mass. Each item has a force that attracts other items to it; Newton called this force gravity. He explained gravity as a force that pulls items to it. The Earth has a gravitational force that pulls items to it. If we drop something, it will fall to the ground. Knowing this helps us predict events: We know that if we drop something, gravity will pull it to the ground. Thus, by using gravity, it is possible to understand the three functions of a theory: organizing, explaining, and predicting.

The social sciences do not have theories developed as clearly as gravity. The role of the social scientist is to use observations to develop theories. Just as Newton used his observations of items falling to the ground to develop gravity, we use our observations to try to develop theories that will predict occurrences in human nature.

There are times when more than one theory is used to explain a particular event, especially when the event is a new experience or phenomenon. When theories are used to predict the relationship between two or more concepts, the process is called *hypothesis building.*

A *hypothesis* is a statement describing the relationship between two concepts. The relationship is logically derived from existing theories. The hypothesis then predicts the observations from the interactions between these two concepts. Hypotheses are expectations about the way things should be in the world if the theoretical expectations are correct.

As scientists, we test hypotheses as part of the research process. The hypothesis predicts a direction or expresses an assumed relationship between variables. It is the observation of the relationship between variables that is used to determine the validity of the hypothesis.

In reality, the hypothesis itself is not tested. The scientist creates an inverse of the hypothesis and tests that. This is called the *null hypothesis.* The hypothesis is stated in positive or affirmative form: "There is a difference between this and that." The null hypothesis, which is tested, is a negative form of that statement: "There is no difference between this and that." The scientist hopes to find sufficient evidence to reject the null hypothesis. By disproving the null hypothesis, scientists then assume that the hypothesis is true.

The process for doing quantitative research just described is another way of expressing the deductive approach to theory construction. However, not all relationships between concepts have been explained by a theory, especially in the social sciences, which are still developing. In addition, many of the theories that currently do exist are not strong predictors of relationships. Therefore, the nature of research in the social sciences is to build theories. Glaser and Strauss (1967) call this the discovery of theory from data, or grounded theory (p. 1). Grounded theory represents an inductive approach to theory construction. It involves qualitative research.

In the inductive approach to theory construction, the researcher analyzes observations that lead to empirical generalizations. With no theories that predict relationships, the researcher observes the interactions between concepts to learn whether any repeated events occur. If such repetitions are found, their presence suggests some generalizable relationship. From this process the researcher develops a theory. However, with no existing theories that predict relationships, this form of research is called exploratory research, which is usually qualitative.

In addition to the exploratory type, there are two other kinds of research to think about: *descriptive* and *explanatory.* Descriptive research, which can be either qualitative or quantitative, records and reports the interaction between factors, regardless of the causal relationship. Explanatory research, which is usually quantitative, confirms the relationship that previous research has described. Because qualitative research relies more on observation than on precise and generalizable statistical findings, qualitative research will be primarily exploratory, with the possibility of some descriptive research methodologies. These types of research are examined later in the chapter; but before moving to the discussion of them, we need to understand the cognitive development of research and then describe the process that an individual follows in conducting a research project.

Research begins when a researcher tries to solve a problem, define an interest, or explain an idea (see Figure 1.3). The researcher then looks at the theoretical concepts that relate to the problem. A *concept* is a mental idea or representation of a class of events or group of objects. Concepts are words that symbolize ideas created by the researcher. For example, if I tell you to close your eyes and visualize a car, each of you will visualize some type of car. However, if I then asked you to describe the car, the answers would be very different depending upon who was responding. One of you may have seen a '57 Chevy, another may have visualized a red Corvette, and a third may have imagined a black BMW. This demonstration shows that everyone seems to have a sense of what the concept of "car" means; however, when the concept is described, there is a lot of variance. Thus, because concepts are invented by researchers, it is important for them to *operationalize* the concept by developing a precise definition.

In thinking about the problem, the researcher identifies a couple of theoretical concepts. Then he or she begins to look at the relationship that exists between these concepts. At this point, the concepts are very abstract; it is hard to observe them because the definition of what is being observed is not precise. As with the car example, no exact definition has been made for exactly what is being observed.

Returning to the homeless question mentioned earlier, the basic definition of a homeless person is someone without a home. However, there is tremendous variance in what that means. Is a battered woman who leaves her home to escape the abuse homeless? Is a minor who runs away from home homeless? Someone whose home burns down is obviously homeless, but what about the person who was

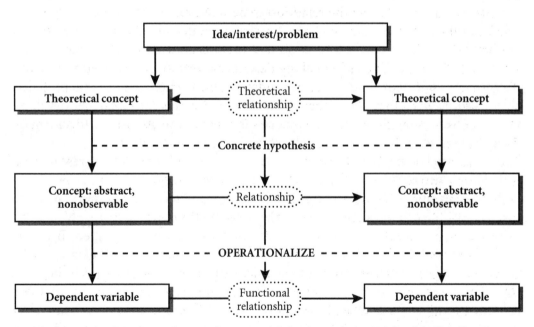

Figure 1.3   Cognitive research map. *(Note: Special thanks to Thomas Holland for helping to conceptualize this model.)*

evicted because of insufficient money? These descriptions differentiate *individuals*, but there are also differences between individuals who are homeless and homeless *families*. Before beginning any research project about homeless people, it is important to define clearly what is meant by homelessness and who is homeless. In many communities, battered women are not considered homeless because they do have a home. Thus, it is important to define with precision the terms that are being used. Accurate definitions are essential for every research project.

To operationalize, the researcher defines the concepts precisely, and then states the assumed relationship between the concepts. This is accomplished by assigning measurable terms to the concept. For example, describing "car" and "homeless person," respectively, as "a black 528e BMW" or "an individual who has not lived at any particular address for 30 or more days" would be ways of operationalizing these concepts. When the researcher has been able to define the concepts clearly, he or she has created a *variable*. A variable is a concept that can be measured.

As problems are really questions about the relationship between concepts, researchers need to understand the nature of the relationship in question. They are faced with looking at two or more variables that have a relationship with each other and they must be able to describe the nature of the relationship.

For example, in thinking about services that address the homeless problem, the homeless shelter comes to mind. But what is the homeless shelter? To operationalize it, the researcher could describe a homeless shelter as an emergency, temporary residence that provides room and board for an individual for no more than 90 days. This definition differentiates individual shelters from family shelters. It also makes clear the nature of the shelter as transitional rather than permanent. To study the relationship between homeless people and an agency that serves them, the operational definitions of homeless people and shelters would be used to begin to explore relationships between the two.

A way of understanding the relationship between variables is like baking a cake. You need the raw ingredients—eggs, flour, sugar, water, and other things—before starting. These raw ingredients are mixed in a bowl, poured into a pan, and baked. The result is a cake. The cake analogy describes a relationship between variables. The eggs, flour, sugar, and water are independent variables. By themselves they stand alone. When mixed together, they interact in a way that creates a cake. The cake then is dependent, or the dependent variable in the study. It is affected by the independent variables; in this case, it would not exist without them. The independent variables, however, can exist quite well with or without the cake. There are also some control variables. These controls are the size of the pan, the length of time the batter is mixed, the baking temperature, and the number of minutes the cake is baked. All these become factors that relate to the quality of the cake.

Answering a research question is similar to baking a cake. A relationship exists between variables. It is up to the researcher to determine which are the independent variables and which are the dependent variables—that is, which ones are affecting the others. Unlike the interactions in making a cake, however, sometimes the relationship among variables is not so clear. This is where the researcher needs to conceptualize—to sit back and reflect on the meaning of the question. The cognitive process of developing a research problem is represented by Figure 1.3.

Returning to the homeless example, the two concepts are homeless people and homeless shelters. If the outcome is that people become housed, then the independent variables become the homeless people and the homeless shelter. The transformation of the homeless person to one who is being housed then becomes the dependent variable. The vehicle to achieve housing is the homeless shelter. However, these services were not defined. Thus, the identification of services to achieve housing would also be independent variables. The dependent variable is the goal or what one hopes to achieve.

This brief example shows that independent and dependent variables are not clear in some social science questions. In addition, the type of research (exploratory, descriptive, or explanatory) you do will determine how you look at the relationship between independent and dependent variables. That is why you must understand the cognitive nature of research within the context of the research process.

The Research Process

To this point, we have discussed research as a form of scientific inquiry that provides a methodology for answering questions. However, we have not discussed the research process. Figure 1.4 depicts this process. From the figure we see that there are two coexisting processes. One is the logical and cognitive process and the second is the technical process of doing research. The logical and cognitive process involves the first two steps of choosing a problem and forming a hypothesis. The rest of the research cycle is technical. This cycle is applicable for both inductive and deductive approaches to research.

Remember: Research is conducted to answer a question. Therefore, the beginning of any research process is a question or a problem that the researcher wants answered or resolved. The problem may be relevant only to the researcher, but that

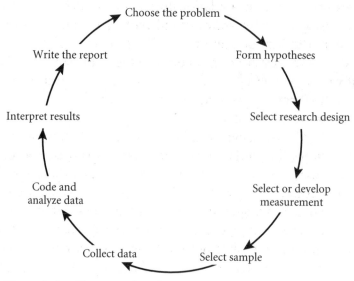

Figure 1.4 The research cycle

is all right as it is the researcher who wants to find the answer. He or she must determine how to do this.

As we have noted, there are two different realities in life: that which is observed and that which is agreed on. As the researcher, you must look at your question and begin a search of existing literature to determine whether the state of knowledge appropriately or adequately answers the question at hand. If you decide that the existing literature answers the question sufficiently, you will choose the deductive approach to test the question. However, if the level of knowledge is not sufficient to resolve the issue, you will follow the inductive approach. Understand that most research questions do not involve a simple either/or resolution, but usually require a combination of the two. Where the qualitative/quantitative debate arises is more a matter of design methodology, which is discussed later.

The next step is to form a hypothesis. This step involves operationalizing the concepts that relate to the problem. Once the concepts have been operationalized and turned into variables, you must identify the relationships that exist between them. As a hypothesis is a statement that defines the relationship between variables that can be tested empirically, it is important that you describe the nature of the relationship. However, there are times when you are not sure what this nature is. Then you have a study without a hypothesis to test. This is an exploratory study. Figure 1.5 briefly shows how to determine the nature of the question and how to translate this decision into a specific type of research study.

Figure 1.5 shows the importance of first understanding the nature of the question being asked. To understand the question, you will go through the logical and creative process of the research cycle to fine-tune the question and the formulation of a hypothesis. In the likelihood that the question represents a new conceptual area, then formulating a hypothesis is not possible and you will choose an exploratory design—the first of three types of qualitative research. Exploratory research involves a systematic process of observing and then analyzing the observations to decide whether there are generalized categories that describe the relationship between variables.

If you are able to describe a relationship between the variables, you will choose a descriptive research design—the second type of design. Descriptive research is used when the researcher can identify relationships between variables but the relationship is still new. Therefore, the state of the art is to describe the relationship. You can do this in several ways, but usually through some type of survey or census of many cases or by conducting single-subject design. Single-subject design takes a single case and measures it over time. The changes that occur are compared to earlier states of that case. Thus, comparisons are made only to the different conditions of that case and not to the larger environment (Barlow & Hersen, 1984). The experimental nature tests relationships that are suggested through the hypothesis. In either survey research or single-subject design, the focus is on describing the nature of the relationship that exists between variables as expressed in a hypothesis.

The third type of research design is explanatory or confirmatory. In this type, the researcher has decided there has been sufficient research to explain the problem but wants to confirm the generalizability to her or his specific question. Therefore, the research confirms the results of existing research.

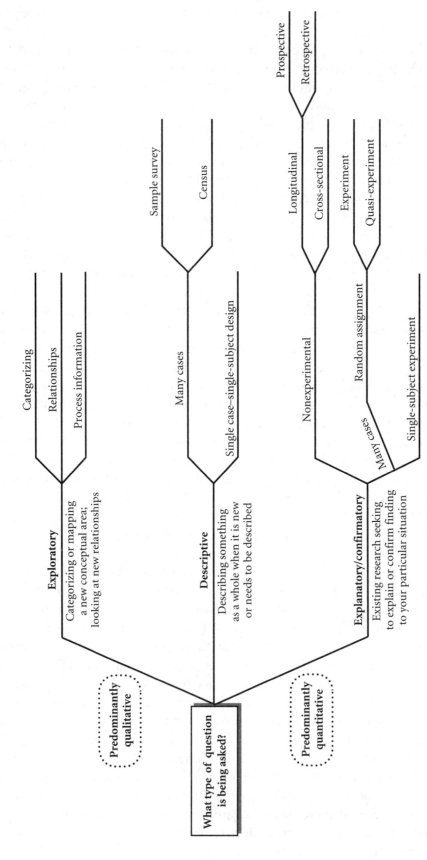

Figure 1.5 Research design decision tree. *(Note: Special thanks to Claudia Coulter.)*

As you can see, the logical procedure is necessary to determine which design is appropriate for the research to be done. I placed the literature review very early in the process because it will help you in developing a hypothesis. In addition, the literature review is essential for revealing the state of knowledge about your particular question and should start early in the process. However, the literature review does not end here. You should check the literature throughout the research process. As you narrow the question, the literature will help you clarify the additional questions that arise. The ongoing review will help to ensure that your study provides relevant information.

Even so, you need to keep a balance between reviewing the literature and actually carrying out the study. Researchers can sometimes become complacent, waiting for someone else to answer their question; in such situations, they rarely find complete and satisfying solutions. That is why I call research a passion, for researchers are truly driven to obtain answers to their question. Conceptualizing is indeed difficult, but once these decisions are made the rest of the research process is purely technical. There is some art to the technique, which is described later.

Now that you as the researcher have gone through the mental gymnastics of forming a hypothesis that has led to a research design, the next step is to develop some criteria for collecting and measuring the data. These steps are techniques that will vary depending on the type of research design selected. Later in the text I go through the specific techniques as they relate to your research, and numerous other texts are available that describe different techniques. The methodology for collecting and measuring data is subject to the rigors of validity and reliability testing.

Once the criterion for measuring the data has been determined, you will decide on the sample frame. This is the selection of the subjects from the population who will help to answer the question under study. Numerous factors affect sampling, and many of these will be dictated by the nature of the question and the type of design you choose.

After the preliminary work has been completed, it is time to collect the data. This is the operationalizing of the study, heavily dictated by the nature of the research question. You will have outlined these methods in the development of the study.

The next two steps will vary dramatically depending on whether the study is exploratory or descriptive or explanatory. Remember that descriptive and explanatory studies test a hypothesis. Therefore, the data collected in them can be coded and analyzed in a way that proves or disproves the hypothesis. Exploratory research does not have a hypothesis that shows relationships between variables. Therefore, the coding and analyzing of the data are very different from that used in the other two types of research. It is from the analysis of exploratory data that relationships between variables emerge.

This leads to the interpretation of the data. Again, the nature of interpretation will derive from the type of research being conducted. Descriptive and explanatory research will interpret why or why not the relationship happened the way it was hypothesized. The results of exploratory research will be interpreted to suggest relationships leading to hypotheses that can be tested by descriptive research.

Finally, it is important to write a report. What good is new information if you just keep it to yourself? The purpose for doing research is to acquire new information or to solve a problem. Because you were solving a problem that concerned you, you could assume that someone else was probably also interested in the problem. Therefore, it is important to share your discovery with the world. Because knowledge in the social sciences is not complete, many questions are still unanswered or have incomplete solutions. Therefore, it is important for all social science researchers to share their knowledge.

The research cycle is truly a cycle. We conduct research to answer questions and to add to the knowledge of our field. We build on the research of others, who take our results to explore further. Exploratory research is used to identify relationships between variables. Descriptive research describes the nature of the relationship more fully. And explanatory research confirms the generalizability of the relationship to the larger population. Therefore, it is a continuous cycle where new knowledge leads to new questions that someone wants to answer. That is why I do not like the terminology of a qualitative/quantitative research debate. There is no debate. Qualitative research uses observations to build theories that will predict future occurrences of those observations. Quantitative research then tests those theories. One form builds on the other. Research methodology embraces many different ways of gaining knowledge. All methods have purpose and value. The ebb and flow between the two major methodologies need to be understood.

The remainder of this Tool Kit provides you with a step-by-step approach to completing a research project. Research is a logical process, and in any logical process, if the task can be parceled into manageable steps, there is an increased likelihood that the goal will be achieved. Therefore, the Tool Kit is a way to make the task of doing research manageable.

One last thought before we get started: Research is not a separate, isolated discipline but one that is integrated throughout the social sciences. The steps presented here are very similar to the steps followed in working with client systems in identifying solutions to problems. The steps may not be so specifically spelled out; however, the process is the same. For example, when you do interviews you are actually gathering data. An assessment involves defining concepts and operationalizing them. A literature review is done by looking at other cases that may be similar to the one before you. Contracting and performing an intervention is the same as conducting a research project in which you measure the results to determine whether the intervention was successful. Therefore, research is just a technical term for our interactions with client systems. We may have different definitions for client systems—whether micro, mezzo, or macro forms of practice—but research is a systematic approach to the work we do with them.

CHAPTER TWO

The Question

The most important part of any research study is the question. Researchers do not begin a project by stating the type of research that they plan to conduct. They undertake a project to solve a problem. It is in developing the question that the researcher is led to decide whether the design will be qualitative or quantitative.

A research question can derive from any problem that the researcher wants answered. The researcher begins by stating the problem in the form of a question. Once the basic question is posed, it can be refined and developed further. Developing the question is a process in itself and is rarely completed on the first attempt. It will be changed and refocused as more information is uncovered about the subject. The worksheets with each chapter reflect that changing and refocusing by asking you to restate the question before beginning each new task.

I can demonstrate with a practical example from qualitative research I conducted about homeless shelters. The initial impetus for the study arose when the Bridgeport area began experiencing an increase in the number of homeless people. The first community reaction was that the city needed to create more shelters to house all the homeless people on the streets. However, a range of questions emerged when the citizens tried to address this social problem: Who are the homeless people? What kind of system should be developed to remedy homelessness? What happens in a homeless shelter to address the problems that led to the person's being homeless? The problem drove the research process to find some answers to these questions. The questions direct the research. In my study, the interest was in building homeless shelters. This led to a research question: What happens in a homeless shelter to address the problems that led to the person's being homeless?

Let's look at the question to see how it relates to a research project. First, look at the question. It is clearly stated: There is a problem about which we are trying to gain information. Second, look at the terms in the question: *homeless shelter, people who are homeless,* and *problems relating to the condition of being homeless.* Before any type of research could begin, these three terms had to be defined in light of the current state of knowledge in this area. For this research, I defined them as follows: *homeless shelter* was part of the social system that provided food and shelter for people who did not have a home or a place to reside. *People who are homeless* were defined as single adults who did not have a permanent or temporary residence in a given 24-hour period. *Problems relating to the condition of being homeless* included a variety of causes—from substance abuse to mental illness to a combination of substance abuse and mental illness and more.

By delineating these general definitions of the terms, I was able to begin the next phase of the research: conducting a literature review to learn the state of information relating to the question. The definitions and the question were just preliminary steps. Through the process I describe, these points are refined into an operational approach to conducting a research study. In the section titled "Select a Researchable Question," there are clues to help you develop your own research question. State as a question the problem you want answered. Look at the question and identify the themes in the question, then define those themes.

▼▼▼

Select a Researchable Question

Select a question of interest to you and express it in a simple, nontechnical, interrogative sentence.

What happens in a homeless shelter to address the problems that led to
the person's being homeless?

Identify the important terms in your question and define them using language as concise as possible.

Term

1. Homeless shelter

2. Problems that lead to one's
becoming homeless

3. Homeless person

4.

5.

Definition

1. An emergency facility that provides
room and board to people without
a home

2. Factors that contribute to loss
of housing

3. Single adult, without a place to
live, who has requested shelter
from a community-based shelter

4.

5.

▼▼▼

Select a Researchable Question

Select a question of interest to you and express it in a simple, nontechnical, interrogative sentence.

_____

_____

_____

_____

Identify the important terms in your question and define them using language as concise as possible.

Term	**Definition**
1. _____	1. _____
_____	_____
_____	_____
_____	_____
2. _____	2. _____
_____	_____
_____	_____
_____	_____
3. _____	3. _____
_____	_____
_____	_____
_____	_____
4. _____	4. _____
_____	_____
_____	_____
_____	_____
5. _____	5. _____
_____	_____
_____	_____
_____	_____

▼▼▼

CHAPTER THREE

Literature Review

After you have stated your research question, you are ready to begin the next step in the research process: the literature review. Different people will suggest doing the literature review at various points in the research process, but I believe it is an ongoing process you should engage in throughout your research. I begin the literature review very early and periodically expand the literature search as new information raises new questions.

Focus Your Review

With the explosion of information technology, it is easy to drown in literature. Therefore, you must focus your review on what you want to find. In the review process, you can easily be sidetracked onto other topics. When this happens, you must ask yourself whether the new question is more interesting than the original one or whether you want to remain with the initial focus. This ongoing decision-making process is the reason you must continually refer to your research question when conducting your literature review.

Has Your Question Been Answered?

You will have identified a number of issues related to your question that you hope the literature will answer for you. First, you want to know whether someone else has already answered your question. If your question has been answered and you are satisfied with the way the research was conducted, there may not be any reason for you to continue with this particular question. In most cases, you will find similarities between existing research and the study you have proposed, but your specific question will not have been answered. With the homeless shelter question, I found research on defining characteristics of homeless people, but none that specifically looked at the homeless shelter.

What Models Have Others Used?

Second, once you find some research that is similar to your question, you want to identify the theories or models that were used by other researchers to answer their questions. Remember that theories provide a framework for predicting observations. Therefore, it is important to identify the theories other researchers used to explain their observations to determine whether these same theories are applicable to your question. Again, in the homeless shelter study, two competing theories emerged from the literature review to explain why people are homeless. One was social systems theory that considered the shelter part of a larger social system to address the needs of homeless people. The other was social support theory. This was identified because homeless people seemed to have an absence of social supports. The assumption in this research was that the shelter can replace those social supports to address the problems of the homeless person. However, there was no information about applying this theory to homelessness. Therefore, I looked at the aging literature for applications of it.

Should You Include Related Questions?

Third, you look at related but less similar research to see what other questions may have emerged from these studies. The issues of poverty and joblessness continued to figure as contributing factors to homelessness. They became important elements to consider in looking at the role of the shelter. In addition, examining other factors helped me to realize that there were differences between single adult and family-oriented shelters. For ease and simplicity, I redefined my population to study only shelters serving single adults. A number of other influencing elements may also be identified from the literature. For example, racism as a possible contributor to homelessness continued to recur, suggested by questions that identified greater proportions of people of color than white people as being homeless. Thus, other factors relating to your question that may be identified through the literature review include issues of race, gender, class, and identity.

Begin with Broad References

This information may be helpful, but how do you begin to do a literature review? Where do you start? As children, we are taught to think horizontally. By that I mean we learn to address questions very broadly. Our first piece of elementary school research was to look up a word in a dictionary. Then we graduated to using an encyclopedia as a reference tool. Dictionaries and encyclopedias provide an overview of many different topics; they do not explore any in depth. They are sufficient for an early research project, but we are in a professional program trying to dig deeply into problem solving. Before we can go very deep, we need to understand the surface. We have to understand the concepts we want to research. We began that process by defining our terms in the research question. But what do those terms really mean? Dictionaries and encyclopedias specific to your field are good places to begin building a general understanding of your research question.

However, to do research successfully, we must be able to think vertically. This process involves narrowing and focusing on the question until we find the answer that satisfies our level of inquiry. The deeper we dig, the more information we find about the problem. There will be points along the research process that will answer parts of the question, but to follow the quest to a thorough conclusion, you need a passion or desire for the answer that will completely satisfy your particular inquiry. Only you can determine when you have a satisfactory answer.

You may also be distracted by side questions. When this happens, you need to keep your question in focus. You may find, however, that one of the side questions is more interesting to pursue than your original question. If you decide to change directions, that is fine. After all, this is your research.

The literature review in the homeless shelter research was very beneficial for me. It helped me narrow my population to single homeless individuals and my definition of the service delivery system to shelters serving single adults. This fine-tuning illustrates what I meant earlier when I said you would develop the research question as you gain more knowledge and information about the subject.

To begin the narrowing process, use the dictionary, encyclopedia, and thesaurus to obtain basic definitions and identify key words that relate to your question. This will not answer specifics but it is a beginning point.

After you have used these reference tools to identify key words, move to an intermediate step of looking at other background sources of information. These may include your textbooks or other general books on the topic. You may also read some annual reviews or other general information such as newspapers or popular magazines. This exploration will help you gain a clearer understanding of how to address your question.

Search the Deeper Sources

Once you feel you have a good understanding of your question, move to other sources of information retrieval. There are many types, including bound copies of abstracts and bibliographies on the subject you are researching. With new technology, there are also easily accessible electronic databases that will help you search many volumes of information in shorter periods of time. These can be very helpful, but you need to know how to use them. You should not sit down at a computer terminal and punch in key words without first looking at the specific thesaurus for that abstracting service. An example is the term *social work*. Most electronic abstracts would see that as two words, *social* and *work*. The database would find all citations that included both words, though not necessarily the phrase *social work*. The search would then follow that pattern of citations with both *social* and *work*. What you identify would probably be off the mark of what you want to find. Therefore, it is important to include the appropriate identifiers for that particular abstract so that the term *social work* would be sought.

You may find several databases that have information about the subject you want to research. However, be careful that the terms mean the same for each database. For example, in searching *homeless* in PsychLit, I found that the citations identified causative factors for homelessness. Sociology abstracts identified social forces leading to homelessness. ERIC identified children coming from homeless families. And MedLine identified citations on medical issues relating to homeless people. Therefore, you need to do some preparation for the search before you begin—another illustration of why it is important to keep your question visible and to start with the question.

The "Literature Search" following is a guide to help you organize your literature review based on your research question.

Literature Search

State your question.

What happens in a homeless shelter to address the problems that led to

the person's being homeless?

Questions You Hope Are Already Answered by Previous Research	Likely Sources Where Articles May Be Found	Key Words
What causes people to become homeless?	Bassuk articles in Scientifiic American	Homeless?
		Shelters
How do homeless shelters operate?	State Dept. of Human Services and federal Health and Human Services literature	
What theoretical framework do shelter staff use in addressing the problems of homeless people?	Child Welfare League of America	
	Social work journals	

Relevant Theories or Models	Authors, Source, and Dates of Relevant Articles
Social systems theory	Rosenberg & Brody (1974), *Systems Serving People: A Breakthrough in Service Delivery*
Social support theory	Warren (1982), *Using Helping Networks*
Senior centers model	Gelfand & Gelfand (1982), *Senior Centers and Social Networks*

Literature Search
(continued)

Other Background Information You Could Use

Urban planning and gentrification
_____

Women's and family shelters
_____
_____

Authors and Articles

Reamer (1989), *The Affordable Housing Crisis and Social Work*
_____

McChesney (1988), *Homeless Families* (a series of articles from Albany)
_____

Race, Gender, and Class Biases from the Literature

Number of minorities who
are homeless
_____
_____

Sources of Information

_____
_____
_____

List other sources that may be relevant to your question.

Systems that address social supports for senior adults
_____

Identify how the literature has defined causal relationships between terms with the independent variable having an effect on the dependent variable. List the variables as defined by the literature.

The literature has discussed a relationship between formal social supports and homelessness: Those who are linked to the formal social support system should have adequate resources to prevent homelessness.
_____

Independent Variable

Social supports
Homeless shelter
_____
_____

Dependent Variable

_____
_____
_____

If necessary, please continue on separate page.

Literature Search

State your question.

_____

_____

_____

_____

Questions You Hope Are Already Answered by Previous Research	**Likely Sources Where Articles May Be Found**	**Key Words**
_____	_____	_____
_____	_____	_____
_____	_____	_____
_____	_____	_____
_____	_____	_____
_____	_____	_____
_____	_____	_____
_____	_____	_____
_____	_____	_____
_____	_____	_____

Relevant Theories or Models	**Authors, Source, and Dates of Relevant Articles**
_____	_____
_____	_____
_____	_____
_____	_____
_____	_____
_____	_____

▼▼▼
Literature Search
(continued)

**Other Background Information
You Could Use**

_____

_____

_____

_____

_____

Authors and Articles

_____

_____

_____

_____

_____

**Race, Gender, and Class Biases
from the Literature**

_____

_____

_____

Sources of Information

_____

_____

_____

List other sources that may be relevant to your question.

_____

_____

Identify how the literature has defined causal relationships between terms with the independent variable having an effect on the dependent variable. List the variables as defined by the literature.

_____

_____

_____

_____

Independent Variable

_____

_____

_____

Dependent Variable

_____

_____

_____

If necessary, please continue on separate page.

CHAPTER FOUR

Justification of the Study

An overriding question in any research process is the justification of the study. You are conducting the study because it is of interest to you, but is it of interest to anyone else or the field? These are important considerations, as every field is requesting more information on accountability. The recurring questions are these: Who cares? What is the relevance? How important is the correct answer? What are the implications of alternatives? They must be answered before you undertake the research study. In addition, as funding moves away from research and toward providing services, these questions become important in demonstrating a link between research and practice.

The questions in the preceding paragraph were very important in the study about homeless shelters. For the community, the easy solution to homelessness was to build more shelter beds without looking at what happens in a shelter to address the root problem of homelessness. The community had an immediate problem and wanted an immediate solution. Conducting a study would delay resolution of the problem. Therefore, the answers to these questions had to be thought out very carefully if the community was to be convinced that more information was needed before additional resources were committed to adding more shelter beds. The "Who cares?" question focused on a combination of people. Of course there were the homeless people, but "who" also involved administrators of existing shelters as well as community leaders. The more inclusive you can be in identifying the "who," with an explanation of their role in the project, the greater will be your potential for building support and allies for the research. A general rule of thumb I subscribe to is this: If one person plans a program, you are guaranteed that only one person will show up. It is better to err on the side of inclusion.

Once the "who" has been identified, it is important to answer the other questions in relation to the "who." For example, the goal of the study of homeless shelters was to identify what happens in a homeless shelter to address the problems of people who were homeless, but the relevance of that goal is different for each population group. For homeless people, the aim is to identify an appropriate service delivery system to address their needs. Shelter professionals would see the goal as a way of informing the community of the types of services they provide, with the aim of enhancing potential funding to continue those services. Community leaders would want the information to assist them in establishing criteria for who receives funding for what aspect of the program. These are all legitimate aims related to the needs of the people who want to be informed about the problem that led to the study.

Following is a form, "Justifying the Study," that asks the four questions. Answer them, and then use the answers to write a paragraph supporting your reasons for conducting this study.

Justifying the Study

State your research question, then answer each question.

_____

_____

_____

_____

1. Identify all sources who will be interested in the answer.

_____

_____

_____

_____

2. Describe the relevance of the study for each source.

_____

_____

_____

_____

3. Describe the importance of having the right answer for each.

_____

_____

_____

_____

4. Describe the implications of various possible answers for each source.

_____

_____

_____

_____

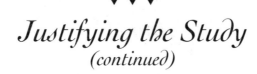

Justifying the Study
(continued)

5. Write a paragraph justifying your study. Consider the questions above but feel free to modify or add to them.

_____

_____

_____

_____

_____

_____

_____

_____

_____

_____

_____

_____

_____

_____

_____

_____

_____

_____

_____

_____

_____

_____

_____

_____

CHAPTER FIVE

Variables

To this point, you have been identifying concepts that relate to your research question. Those concepts, however, were somewhat abstract. Through the literature review you should have begun to obtain some definition for them. Now you need to begin defining them in some measurable way. This process is called *operationalizing.* When you operationalize a concept, you not only define it in measurable terms but you change it into a variable.

Three Types of Variables

There may be three types of variables that relate to your question. First, there are independent variables, presumed to be causal. Second, there are dependent variables that are to be affected by the causal variables. Finally, there are control variables. These are factors that you want to keep constant so you can obtain a true picture of the cause-and-effect relationship between independent and dependent variables.

Think back to the analogy of baking a cake. The raw ingredients are your independent variables. The dependent variable is the cake. The control variables are the oven temperature, the size of the pan, the altitude, and the length of mixing time. These are all factors you control in determining the effect of the independent variables on the dependent variable.

Operationalizing Variables

It is not always as easy to determine independent, dependent, and control variables in a research study. There is the potential for a tremendous amount of variance in terms, and much is determined by how you operationalize the concepts. For example, in the study of homeless shelters, the assumption was this: If the shelter created support mechanisms, there would be a way to address the problems that contributed to the person's becoming homeless. This led to identifying types of *social supports* as the independent variable and *the ways homeless shelters address the problems of homeless people* as the independent variable. Social supports could be broken into formal social supports (linkage to the formal support system established to address the problems) and informal social supports (interaction with friends and family members). The control variables were the characteristics of the shelters (single adult, 24-hour, emergency shelters in the greater Bridgeport area).

It appeared easy to identify the variables and the causal relationship that was being tested. However, the difficulty arose in operationalizing the concepts. There was just not enough information about the concepts in this setting to create specific operational definitions. The lack of operational definitions led to a qualitative research design. That is discussed later. I mention the shift here to demonstrate a common difficulty: For most research questions, the variables can be identified; the problem arises in trying to operationalize or measure those variables.

Operationalizing variables is the process of moving from the abstract to the specific. It involves taking the concept and applying some specific measurements to that concept, turning it into a variable. For example, when the term *homeless shelter* is mentioned, some may visualize a warehouse with rows of cots for people to sleep in and escape from the cold. The term *homeless shelter* is a concept; the description used operationalizes that concept. However, that description may not accurately portray the concepts you are studying. For example, in the homeless shelter study, the concept *homeless shelter* was more accurately described as a 24-hour service delivery system that provided food, shelter, and links to social services for people who were homeless. This definition clearly defines the parameters of what shelters do. However, because the question required a definition of the ways in which shelters addressed the problems of homeless people, the specific issue was how the shelters provide the linking services to other social services that were designed to prevent homelessness. This specificity helped to narrow the focus of the study to examine the way shelters provide those links and to identify barriers that prevent linkage to social services. Thus, by operationalizing a concept and turning it into a variable, you begin to place parameters on an abstract concept. By so doing, you create a method of measuring an abstraction and turning it into an easily defined variable. On the following pages, identify your variables from your research question and define them in measurable terms.

▼▼▼
Variables and Definitions

Identify the independent, dependent, and control variables in your question. Dependent variables are those your study seeks to explain or understand. Independent variables are those you suspect to have an effect on the dependent variables. Control variables are included to enhance the validity of the design by eliminating rival explanations or specifying the conditions under which something occurs.

For each variable, provide an operational definition reflecting how this variable will be observed in this study.

Dependent Variables | **Operational Definition**

The ways homeless shelters address the problems of homeless people

Independent Variables | **Operational Definition**

Homeless shelter

A social service agency that provides room, board, and links to services that were created to provide resources to people in order to prevent episodes of homelessness.

Control Variables | **Operational Definition**

Shelter characteristics:
(a) accommodating only single adults,
(b) located in greater Bridgeport area,
and (c) operating on 24-hour
emergency basis

Single adults with no dependents accompanying them to the shelter

Shelters in the Bridgeport-Fairfield area in Connecticut

Variables and Definitions

Identify the independent, dependent, and control variables in your question. Dependent variables are those your study seeks to explain or understand. Independent variables are those you suspect to have an effect on the dependent variables. Control variables are included to enhance the validity of the design by eliminating rival explanations or specifying the conditions under which something occurs.

For each variable, provide an operational definition reflecting how this variable will be observed in this study.

Dependent Variables   **Operational Definition**

_____   _____

_____   _____

_____   _____

_____   _____

Independent Variables   **Operational Definition**

_____   _____

_____   _____

_____   _____

_____   _____

_____   _____

_____   _____

Control Variables   **Operational Definition**

_____   _____

_____   _____

_____   _____

_____   _____

_____   _____

_____   _____

_____   _____

_____   _____

CHAPTER SIX

Hypotheses

A hypothesis is a probability statement about the relationship between variables. With the cake we described earlier, if all the ingredients interact appropriately and the controls are maintained, your efforts will be deliciously rewarded. The probability is high that the cake will be good each time you make it, as long as you follow the directions.

Developing a Conceptual Hypothesis

The probability of successful repetition in the social sciences is not as high as with baking a cake. That is why we continue to explore research questions about interactions. We can assume certain inferences from the literature. These inferences then lead to a hypothesis that you want to test.

For example, in the homeless shelter study, the literature about informal supports in senior centers described a positive correlation between informal supports and participant well-being (the more informal supports people had, the healthier they were). Second, the literature on people who were homeless described them as being devoid of supports, both formal and informal. Therefore, it was assumed that if supports could be provided, they could be used to address the problems of people who were homeless as they had been used for problems of the elderly. This, then, was a conceptual hypothesis.

Difficulty in Operationalizing
a Conceptual Hypothesis

The difficult part was operationalizing the conceptual hypothesis. On the one hand, quantifying the number of supports, both formal and informal, through a counting system was easy. However, that did not identify the *quality* of that support. In addition, there was a problem with determining the role of the shelter in creating supports that will last. The shelter can make a referral, but is there any guarantee that the person referred will act on that referral? As you can begin to see, the research question about the role of shelters in addressing the problems of people who were homeless led to further questions. The beginning phase was quantifiable and did have a hypothesis: A combination of formal and informal social support provided by the homeless shelter will address the problems of people who are homeless. However, the findings from the initial phase of the study led to other questions where there was no hypothesis. These other questions, with no specific variables or measures, needed to be answered through an exploratory study, which changed the direction of the original study from measuring social supports to identifying factors within the shelter that address the problems that led the individual to the homeless incident. This shift illustrates why research is a fluid process and changes as new information is acquired. It demonstrates the importance of constantly restating your question and later your hypothesis. The goal was to generate initial insights into the nature of the relationship between the shelter and the guests. None of the information obtained earlier was helpful in answering these questions; it only confirmed the need to conduct the study. Many times, quantitative research creates questions that need to be answered through a qualitative study, as happened with the homeless shelter study.

To the best of your ability, look at the relationships between variables and develop a hypothesis. Use the following form as a guide in the development of your hypothesis.

Hypotheses

Hypotheses require you to predict an answer to your question based on knowledge of the field, logical analysis, and/or anecdotal observations. Purely exploratory or descriptive studies do not require formal hypotheses. Even so, it is wise to commit yourself to a set of expectations regarding results.

State your question.

What happens in a homeless shelter to address the problems that led to
the person's being homeless?

_____

_____

Describe how the variables in your question relate to each other.

Social supports	is related to	adequate resources to provide for shelter
Social supports	is related to	assisting the elderly in leading productive lives
Informal social supports	is related to	family and friends who can provide for people in need
Loss of supports	is related to	homelessness

Therefore (independent variable is related to the dependent variable):

Linking people to formal and informal social supports will address the
problem of homelessness.

_____

_____

_____

Hypotheses
(continued)

Initial Statement of Hypotheses

Conceptual hypothesis:

Formal and informal social supports can be developed and used to address
the problems of people who are homeless.

Operational hypothesis:

The linkage of formal supports, such as general assistance and Medicaid, and
the development of an informal social support system, such as connecting to
family and friends, will assist in providing the basic needs (food and shelter)
for the homeless person.

Are there any alternative relationships or explanations that serve as competing or
rival hypotheses?

There are underlying factors leading to homelessness over and above the
loss of social supports.

Revise your hypotheses, considering (if possible) specific competing alternatives
to the hypothesized relationships.

The reasons a person becomes homeless are more complex than just a loss
of social supports and require more in-depth exploration (leading to an
exploratory study).

Hypotheses

Hypotheses require you to predict an answer to your question based on knowledge of the field, logical analysis, and/or anecdotal observations. Purely exploratory or descriptive studies do not require formal hypotheses. Even so, it is wise to commit yourself to a set of expectations regarding results.

State your question.

_____

_____

_____

_____

Describe how the variables in your question relate to each other.

_____   is related to   _____

_____   _____

_____   _____

_____   is related to   _____

_____   _____

_____   _____

_____   is related to   _____

_____   _____

_____   _____

_____   is related to   _____

_____   _____

_____   _____

_____   _____

Therefore (independent variable is related to the dependent variable):

_____

_____

_____

_____

_____

Hypotheses
(continued)

Initial Statement of Hypotheses

Conceptual hypothesis:

_____
_____
_____
_____

Operational hypothesis:

_____
_____
_____
_____
_____
_____

Are there any alternative relationships or explanations that serve as competing or rival hypotheses?

_____
_____
_____
_____

Revise your hypotheses, considering (if possible) specific competing alternatives to the hypothesized relationships.

_____
_____
_____
_____
_____
_____

▼▼▼

CHAPTER SEVEN

Research Design

To this point we have discussed the reason for the study, the variables, the relationship between variables, and hypotheses. Now you are ready to decide the type of study you will conduct.

How to Select a Design

As noted, some studies do not have hypotheses; these are better suited for exploratory designs. In these instances, you use your observations, experiences, and interactions to define a process of intervention that can be tested at a later time. These designs are very individualized with small sample sizes that provide some insight to what is happening.

Other studies are explanatory: They explain a relationship between variables. In an explanatory study you test a hypothesis you defined earlier. You can do this in a number of ways. There is a true experimental design. Using one, however, is very difficult in the social sciences because you are dealing with human subjects. In recent history, the human subjects study closest to a real experimental design was a project that sequestered people in a biosphere for a number of years to see how they would survive. There are different ways to collect data, however, that may be quasi-experimental; that is, they still use an experimental design but do not have all the controls of a true experiment. Other types of designs commonly used in the social sciences are survey, single-subject, or a combination of these. Human service workers are quite adept at designing research projects that will answer their question of interest.

Qualitative or Quantitative?

You must also decide whether you will use qualitative or quantitative methods in conducting your research. The difference is in the type of information you will be measure. Quantitative measures are a way to count information. Closed (forced or limited choice response) surveys provide a good way to collect quantitative data.

Qualitative research involves the use of participant observation for the researcher to understand the relationship taking place between variables. Participant observation is really two different techniques and can be perceived as a continuum. Some individuals collect data as complete observers and have no interaction whatsoever with the target system. Others collect data through active involvement with the target system. Then there are those who combine being a participant with observing the nature of the interactions, gaining insights into the sights, smells, tastes, and feel of the interactions with the target system. Participant observation is a tool used by many anthropologists in their data collection and provides a richness to this type of research that can only be gained through the process.

For the homeless shelter study, I used qualitative measures that included field notes and interviews to determine the relationships among the shelter, the guests, and the staff. I was not sure of these relationships prior to the study, so the hypothesis was vague. The study was used to identify relationships that could be tested at a later time using quantitative measures. A general rule of thumb is this: If what you want measured is clear and defined, use quantitative measures. If you are uncertain about the nature of the relationship, use qualitative measures.

One form of research builds on the other. Therefore, both quantitative and qualitative research measures are important in social work. Remember that because the relationship between variables is clear in a quantitative study, the information is easier to analyze at the analysis stage of the study—the back end. A lot of thought goes into the study before you reach that point, but the data are definitely easier to analyze.

Qualitative research is the opposite. Because the relationship between variables is vague, the questions that you want to test are generalized. This means you have many open-ended questions, and from the answers to them you try to identify trends. The front end of this type of research is easier, but the back end or the analysis phase requires much work. In analysis the researcher must sift through mountains of information to identify trends between sources of data. Focus groups and interviews are some of the data sources that may be used.

Overview of Research Design

Here is a brief overview of the different types of designs currently being used. A more comprehensive description appears in your research text, whichever one you are using.

To provide some of the basic components of an experimental design while being sensitive to human subjects, social scientists use a quasi-experimental design. This provides the basic concepts of experimentation (with experimental and control groups), but the researcher does not have the total control over the environment that could guarantee similarities between experimental and control subjects as in a true experimental design.

Probably the most widely used type of research design in social sciences is the survey. Surveys provide a series of closed-ended questions and can be administered to large groups of people. The way the questions are stated can demonstrate relationships between variables. Surveys can be designed to uncover a variety of interactions between variables. There is an art to survey research because the response rate is usually low. To obtain reliability and validity in survey research, it is necessary to use large samples to guarantee that responses will be generalizable. This is needed because response rates to surveys are generally low.

Many practitioners use research methodologies to determine changes within their clients. This usually takes the form of single-subject design. Simply, a single-subject design examines an intervention with a single client. Single-subject design is a way to measure the effectiveness of an intervention with a particular client. In this type of research, baseline data are collected prior to the intervention. Change in the client's behavior or condition is measured after the intervention and compared with the pre-intervention data to determine the effect of the treatment. Your past relationship with the client acts as the control in helping to determine whether the change can be attributed to your intervention.

There are also designs in which there is no interaction with clients. These can be historical designs that look at information. In this type of qualitative study, you look at information to see whether certain trends may have appeared but were missed earlier. I began the homeless shelter study by looking at case records of shelter guests to determine the nature of the relationship between the shelter, the staff, and the guest. This would be a type of historical design. There are many other types of designs, too numerous to be discussed in this Tool Kit. If none of these seems to fit your study, look in your research book for different designs. You can also be creative and develop your own research design that would surely be right for your needs. "Selecting the Research Design" will give you a starting point in finding the appropriate design for your research project.

Selecting the Research Design

The design of the research refers to the way relationships are to be studied. Choices among designs will always require compromises between the practical and the ideal. Well-designed research, like anything well crafted, should be more efficient and better suited to your needs than a haphazard approach. Poorly designed research may be inefficient or, even worse, may make legitimate analysis of the data impossible.

Determine, in general, what kind of design is most practical and suitable for your study. Choose a design, describe its structure, and then discuss the pros and cons of the design you selected. But first, state your hypothesis:

The reasons that a person becomes homeless are more complex than

just a loss of social supports and require in-depth exploration (leading to

an exploratory study).

Select a research design (quasi-experimental, survey, single-subject, historical, other).

As there is no hypothesis that demonstrates relationships between the selected

variables, then the study will be exploratory.

Describe the structure of the design. If it is easier to diagram the design, do so on a separate sheet of paper.

The study will involve four sources of data: case records, participant observation,

guest interviews, and staff interviews.

Selecting the Research Design
(continued)

Discuss the pros and cons of the design.

This design will provide background information relating to the information that each shelter has on each guest and will provide an understanding of the milieu within each shelter. The interviews will tap the understanding of the "qualified observers," those most informed about the homeless experience and effective mechanisms to address the problems. On the positive side, this design provides an overview of the problem, and the multiple data sources assist in triangulating, or verifying, information. Because the existing hypotheses and theories about this population and the systems serving them are limited, this type of design permits exploration of the information in the broadest sense.

There is also a negative element about this design. An exploratory study is very open. Consequently there are few checks on validity and reliability. To address the problems of validity and reliability in a qualitative study, the number of researchers collecting and analyzing the data is often limited to one. This helps to provide consistency to the information that is being collected. However, limiting the number of researchers also limits the sample size. One goal in qualitative research is to collect data until the themes repeat themselves consistently; this is called *data saturation*. If the number of researchers is restricted, it may not be possible to collect data until saturation is attained.

▼▼▼
Selecting the Research Design

The design of the research refers to the way relationships are to be studied. Choices among designs will always require compromises between the practical and the ideal. Well-designed research, like anything well crafted, should be more efficient and better suited to your needs than a haphazard approach. Poorly designed research may be inefficient or, even worse, may make legitimate analysis of the data impossible.

Determine, in general, what kind of design is most practical and suitable for your study. Choose a design, describe its structure, and then discuss the pros and cons of the design you selected. But first, state your hypothesis:

_____

_____

_____

_____

Select a research design (quasi-experimental, survey, single-subject, historical, other).

_____

_____

_____

_____

Describe the structure of the design. If it is easier to diagram the design, do so on a separate sheet of paper.

_____

_____

_____

_____

_____

_____

_____

_____

_____

Selecting the Research Design
(continued)

Discuss the pros and cons of the design.

CHAPTER EIGHT

Sampling

Ideally, you would study the entire universe to obtain an answer to your question, but that is not realistic. *Sampling* is the term used to define that part of the universe you will use to answer your research question. It is important that your sample is selected appropriately. For example, in the homeless shelter study, the topic could have been approached in many different ways. I limited the research to single-adult shelters for men, creating a population consisting of single-adult, male, homeless shelters. Even within that limiting process, the identified universe or population has different segments. Specifically, there were shelter guests, staff, funders, the community, and street people who are potential guests. I chose to limit that segment to the two populations of shelter guests and staff. It was inappropriate for me to interview street people, even though they were homeless, as they did not see the shelter as a source of help. Therefore, the initial approach to sampling requires a logic to define your particular part of the universe that will appropriately answer your question.

Size of Sample

Not only is whom you sample important, sample size is also critical to the information you collect. The larger your sample, the more data you will have relating to your question, but is a very large sample realistic? There are costs, in money, time, and resources, associated with collecting data from a sample. In addition, there is also the accessibility question. To be realistic means to take these factors into consideration and select a sample size that is manageable given the resources available for your study. If you are a single researcher, identify a sample size that you can manage in your life.

Representativeness of Sample

Given these factors, the researcher then decides to choose a sample that will be representative of the universe to be studied. Again, the homeless shelter study had some essential limitations that helped with sampling. First, I realized that I could not study all shelters; there were too many different types to address the different classifications of homeless people. Therefore, I focused on single-adult emergency shelters. Second, there are homeless shelters all over the country; however, I could not study every shelter so I decided to use a geographic limitation and study shelters in Bridgeport and Fairfield, Connecticut. Third, there are potentially hundreds of people who use the shelters, but I wanted to collect the data in a timely manner that would be manageable for me. Because I had chosen a design that involved various data sources, I was able to use various sample sizes.

Sampling Frames

These factors were part of the *sampling frame* that led to my selection of two single-adult emergency shelters. A sampling frame identifies the elements in the population that contribute to the selection of the specific population. The two shelters selected provided over 30,000 bed nights per year serving over 3,000 different individuals. However, I did not want to collect data for an entire year so I chose to look at the shelter population during the three busiest months of the year, the winter. That was fine for the historical data collection, which involved reviewing case files; however, it would be difficult for the interview aspect of the data collection. Therefore, I chose to limit the number of interviews I conducted at each shelter. I used a random sampling technique to select my sample of guests at each shelter. My assumption was that randomly selecting guests would give me a selection of people with many different reasons for being homeless and therefore a wide range of opinions about the role of the shelter in addressing the problems that led to their homelessness.

I also identified shelter staff as an expert source of data for the study. Again, I did not have the opportunity to interview every staff person so I did a purposive sampling of the staff. Because I wanted to get the perceptions of senior staff as well as new staff members, I purposefully selected staff from each category I identified as important to my data collection.

The fourth source of data I used was participant observation. Ideally, it would have been best for me to have moved into each shelter for a time to get a flavor of what happens during a shelter stay. Realistically, this was not possible. To get as true a picture as possible of what happens in the shelter, it was important to sample all segments of the day as well as to sample days of the week in which to observe and participate in the activities of shelter life.

This brief description shows how I used various sampling frames to identify each source of data. It presents sampling as something that is realistic to the circumstances of the particular study and represents a logic for obtaining the information to enhance reliability and validity of the study.

Sampling is the best method to define a generalizable population that will answer your question. The pages on sampling will help you determine the sample for your study.

Sampling

State your hypothesis.

The reasons that a person becomes homeless are more complex than just a loss of social supports and require in-depth exploration (leading to an exploratory study).

What populations or sources of data will best describe the relationships in your hypothesis?

Case records of shelter guests, interviews with shelter guests, and interviews with shelter staff

How do these populations or sources define the relationship beyond your sample? (generalization of results)

These populations would be classified as "qualified observers" as they are themselves experiencing the homeless situation. Each person would be able to describe the experience based on his or her own experience. The information is unique and specific to the individual's experience. The analysis will suggest elements of the homeless condition that could be tested for generalizability to the larger homeless population.

Are there differences between your proposed sample and the characteristics of the population you are studying?

Because this is an exploratory study, I can't answer this question until the data are gathered and analyzed.

Sampling
(continued)

Describe resource limitations that may affect your sample size.

Because I am the only researcher involved in the study, the number of people I can interview and the length of time I can spend in each shelter are limited. However, the nature of the data sources should compensate for these limitations.

What is the potential population size?

I plan to interview five guests in each shelter and two staff members. In addition, I will experience life in the shelter by making sure that I am present during each shift and a representation of all days of the week.

What sampling frame will you use?

The sampling frame will be single adult males who have been in the shelter more than five days. In addition, English-speaking guests will be used because of my limitations as the interviewer. I will interview one new staff person (employed at the shelter for less than three months) and one veteran (employed at the shelter for two or more years).

How will you select your sample?

Staff sample will be selected based on the criteria mentioned above. The guest sample will be selected based on participant observation and willingness of the guests to participate. In addition, I will consider staff recommendations when selecting guests to be interviewed.

What is a prudent sample size?

The realistic sample size is five guests at each shelter and two staff members at each shelter, as this is what a single researcher can manage in a reasonable amount of time.

Sampling
(continued)

What variables will be controlled in your sample?

The sample will be controlled by the minimum length of time that the guests have
to be in the shelter before they can be interviewed. This will be a minimum of five
days. This time provides opportunity for the guest to be stabilized in the shelter
before he is asked questions about the role and function of the shelter in
addressing the problems that led to homelessness.

Are there any class, race, or gender biases represented by your sample?

The sample will be representative of race issues within the shelter. Only
single adults will be interviewed at this time to maintain uniformity in the
population.

How will you address these biases for your study?

Race and gender biases will conform with the normal perceptions associated
with who is homeless.

Describe your final sample.

The final sample will consist of ten single adults—five from each shelter—
representing the racial differences of each shelter. Four staff members—two
from each shelter—will be interviewed. The staff will represent one new staff
member and one veteran staff member for each shelter. This represents different
perspectives of staff within each shelter.

Sampling

State your hypothesis.

_____
_____
_____
_____

What populations or sources of data will best describe the relationships in your hypothesis?

_____
_____
_____
_____
_____

How do these populations or sources define the relationship beyond your sample? (generalization of results)

_____
_____
_____
_____
_____
_____
_____
_____

Are there differences between your proposed sample and the characteristics of the population you are studying?

_____
_____
_____
_____
_____

Sampling
(continued)

Describe resource limitations that may affect your sample size.

_____

_____

_____

_____

What is the potential population size?

_____

_____

_____

_____

What sampling frame will you use?

_____

_____

_____

_____

How will you select your sample?

_____

_____

_____

_____

What is a prudent sample size?

_____

_____

_____

_____

Sampling
(continued)

What variables will be controlled in your sample?

_____

_____

_____

_____

_____

_____

_____

Are there any class, race, or gender biases represented by your sample?

_____

_____

_____

_____

How will you address these biases for your study?

_____

_____

_____

_____

Describe your final sample.

_____

_____

_____

_____

_____

_____

_____

CHAPTER NINE

Research Protocol

Now that you have decided on a design for the research and know how you will select the sample, you need to discuss what you will do next. For example, in the shelter study, I wanted to see what happens in a shelter to address the problems that led people to become homeless. I selected two shelters so I could compare their services. Therefore, data needed to be collected from each shelter. Using two data sources allowed me to compare shelters and services in how each shelter addressed the problems of its guests.

Charting the Study

Research protocol is just a description of what will happen to the sample in collection. It is the beginning of a description of the research. Sometimes a flowchart or a diagram is helpful to demonstrate the order of the research. I used four sources of data in the homeless study, and the sequencing of the data collection was very important because earlier data was the base on which later data would build. The study was qualitative. However, I used the quantitative data to drive the open-ended questions of the interviews. A flow diagram of the study looked like this:

Review case records → Observe participants → Interview guests → Interview staff

This model was implemented at each shelter.

Safeguards

Because funding for the study was negligent and to protect against interresearcher bias, I alone collected data for the study. I wanted to do the interviewing so that little time would elapse between data gathering at the two shelters. Because there is some mobility by homeless people between shelters and to prevent overlap in the sample, I wanted to make sure the data were collected from both shelters during the same time period.

Now, use the guide sheets and add a research protocol to your study.

Developing the Research Protocol
or Procedure

State your hypothesis.

The reasons a person becomes homeless are more complex than just a
loss of social supports and require in-depth exploration (leading to an
exploratory study).

How will you use your sample?

The sample will be experts about the homeless situation, qualified by their
individual experiences. The information will be gathered from the sample
through interviews.

Provide a flowchart or diagram showing what will happen to your participants.

Review case records → Observe participants → Interview guests → Interview staff

Who will gather the data, and how? (Add a time frame.)

As the sole researcher, I will gather all the data. First, I will spend about a week in
a shelter to review all the case records. Then I will spend about a month at the
shelter, covering various different days and shifts throughout the day. My role
during this phase will be that of participant observer and will be used to gain an
understanding of the shelter milieu. Then I will conduct the guest interviews.
When the guest interviews are completed I will conduct the staff interviews.
This process will be repeated at the second shelter.

▼▼▼

Developing the Research Protocol
or Procedure

State your hypothesis.

_____

_____

_____

_____

How will you use your sample?

_____

_____

_____

_____

Provide a flowchart or diagram showing what will happen to your participants.

Who will gather the data, and how? (Add a time frame.)

_____

_____

_____

_____

_____

_____

_____

_____

CHAPTER TEN

Bias

Errors in your data collection and analysis can ruin your study. To avoid these errors, you must anticipate possible sources of error prior to conducting your research. This is part of the critical thinking of the research process—to anticipate the problems and resolve them before they become real. Once you identify the potential sources of error, you can begin to control for them.

Sources of Bias

There are eight possible sources of error to consider. These include historical events, maturation, repeated measures, instrument decay, statistical regression, subject selection, loss of subjects, and investigator bias. Some of these errors can occur in all research models; some may apply only to either a quantitative or a qualitative study. However, it is important to ask yourself questions relating to all eight in conceptualizing your study.

Checking for Bias

Again we will use the homeless study that has been referenced throughout this text as an example in checking for the various types of errors. The first one we examine is the historical error.

Historical error results from events, such as personnel changes, environmental events, or interference by nonparticipants, that may take place during the data collection phase and may affect the study results. The problem relates to the historical event contributing to the change rather than the specific nature of the intervention. One way to eliminate this source of error is to restrict data collection to a single time. Within the homeless study I conducted, actually living in the shelter was the intervention I was testing, so this type of error was not a problem. It would have been problematic if a guest had not had a consistent stay at the shelter. I was able to control for this, however, through design and the limits that I placed on subject selection.

Maturation error may result when subjects are to be observed over time. This type of error is a result of normal changes that might occur merely by the normal developmental and growth issues that we experience each day. Maturation was also not a source of error because I was interested in seeing how living in the shelter would affect the lives of the guests. I expected to see some change as a result of the guests' experience in the shelter or their maturation.

Repeated measures error results when the same measurements are used repeatedly on subjects. The nature of the error arises because subjects may remember past responses, thus not giving an accurate response to the question as being asked at this time; they may be complacent in responding to the measure this time since it was repeated from a previous time; the procedures may be relaxed because the measurement is being repeated and there are expectations that subjects will remember the procedures. Repeated measures were not a concern because I did not use any standard measure that would influence guest responses. There was some concern about my repeated contact with guests, though. Because I was not a member of the staff, a guest could change as a result of my contact with him. I tried to avoid this error by attempting to blend into the shelter experience before beginning my interviews, which would unavoidably call attention to me. Once I began interviewing guests, I tried to limit my contact with them. The problem continued to persist with the staff because I did have constant contact with them. As it could not be avoided, I had to accept this as a possible source of error and explain it in the results section of the study report.

Instrument decay may occur when using test equipment that may wear out, when observers become bored by the routine, or when investigators short-cut protocols. As a social scientist interested in assessing your work, it is important to anticipate any of these concerns. I tried using a tape recorder that died half-way through the interview. From that point on, I chose not to use one. I also established a manageable number of interviews so I would not get bored or short-cut protocols. It is important to know your own strengths and design your data collection procedure appropriately.

Statistical regression can become an error concern if subjects are chosen because they lie at the extremes of a distribution (e.g., extreme anxiety, low compliance with therapy). However, if you narrow your population to focus solely on those who lie within the extremes, then it can be assumed that within that narrow population there will be normal distribution. By so doing, this will cause all subsequent measurements to be more nearly average, for purely statistical reasons.

Subject selection errors result when assignment of subjects to experimental and control groups makes one group of subjects unintentionally different from other groups. Subject selection was an area of concern. Because I am not multilingual, I limited my sample to men who spoke English. This could be seen as an ethnic bias as it limited my ability to collect data from a full range of guests. In reality, I did try to reach all ethnic groups, with the limitation that the participants had to speak English. I also felt that I compensated for that liability by the methods I used in collecting data. By reviewing all case files, I gained an overview of the entire population at each shelter. With statistical analysis I was able to ascertain any major differences between samples. Through this process, I discovered that there were minimal differences between English-speaking and non-English-speaking guests.

Error can also arise as a result of loss of subjects. The error results because it changes the nature of the experimental samples. The sample that remains may be different from the one initially selected. Because of the perceived transient nature of the homeless population, loss of subjects was a concern. I structured the data in two ways to address this issue. First, by looking at case records I was able to address everyone who came into the shelter. Second, for interviewing, I identified guests who had been in the shelter long enough to be able to reflect adequately the nature of their experiences there. Again, by anticipating the concerns you can begin to address these issues by the design. This also related to loss of subjects since I only did one interview per person. Thus, if a person left the shelter, I at least had their intake file to provide an overview to the larger demographic nature of the shelter.

Investigator bias may result if you influence subjects in their action through your attention, attitude, or interactions with them. Probably the biggest concern in doing qualitative research is investigator bias. I addressed this by being the only person doing the interviews. In this way, if there was bias, it would be consistent for the entire sample. I addressed this possibility in the section of the study that was a discussion of the data.

Investigator bias also could lead to bias relating to gender, race, or class. If your study restricts the population because of one of these factors, it is important that you explain the rationale behind these limitations. As stated, I did not limit the homeless study because of my bias toward any ethnic groups but because of my handicap in not being multilingual; this was my reason for restricting participants to those who spoke English. In addition, because the largest segment of the homeless population was single adult males, I explored that population exclusively. There are differences between them and single homeless women and homeless families that could be explored in future studies.

The pages titled "Eliminating Procedural Bias" identify the eight potential sources of error. Take some time and think about the problems that may arise in your study in relation to these eight types of error and respond appropriately.

▼▼▼
Eliminating Procedural Bias

Bias refers to sources of systematic error that may affect study results. Unless adequately controlled, bias may render your results noninterpretable. With a general protocol in mind, give specific attention to each of the following potential sources of bias. The design should evolve as you add controls for the most serious of these. Those mentioned here are adapted from *Experimental and Quasi-Experimental Design for Research* by D. T. Campbell and J. C. Stanley, 1966, Chicago, Rand McNally.

State your hypothesis.

_____

_____

_____

_____

1. *Effects of historical events.* Anticipate events, such as personnel changes, environmental events, interference by nonparticipants, or others, that will take place during your data collection phase and which might affect the results. Describe the problem and how you will address it.

_____

_____

_____

_____

_____

2. *Effects of maturation.* If participants are to be observed over time, are there changes that might result merely by normal development, growth, natural course of illness, and so on? Describe the problem and how you will address it.

_____

_____

_____

_____

_____

Eliminating Procedural Bias
(continued)

3. *Effects of repeated measurement.* If the same measurements are repeated on participants, will participants likely remember past responses, prepare differently for the next session, or relax procedures? Describe the problem and how you will address it.

_____

_____

_____

_____

_____

4. *Instrument decay.* Is it likely that test equipment will wear out, observers will get bored, protocols will get short-cut by investigators, and so on? Describe the problem and how you will address it.

_____

_____

_____

_____

_____

5. *Effects of statistical regression.* If participants are chosen because they lie at the extremes of a distribution (e.g., extreme anxiety, low compliance with therapy), subsequent measurements will tend to be more nearly average, for purely statistical reasons. Describe how you will select to avoid this problem.

_____

_____

_____

_____

_____

Eliminating Procedural Bias
(continued)

6. *Participant selection.* Is there anything in the selection of your sample or assignment of participants to groups that makes one group of participants unintentionally different from other groups—for example, does your study represent bias toward race, gender, class, sexual preference, or social desirability? Describe how you will avoid the problem.

_____

_____

_____

_____

_____

7. *Loss of participants.* Participants lost to attrition may be different from those who remain. How does your study control for this possibility? Describe how you will avoid the problem.

_____

_____

_____

_____

_____

8. *Investigator bias.* How will you avoid influencing participants by your attention, attitude, and so on? Describe how you will avoid the problem.

_____

_____

_____

_____

_____

▼▼▼

CHAPTER ELEVEN

Data

Data are the heart of the study. They are the pieces of information you collect and use to answer your question.

Collecting Data

Data can be collected through specific instruments, observations of behavior, interviews, or any source of information that can help to define the variables in your study. For example, numerous commercial testing measures are available that will test aspects of behavior. Some sources you could use in identifying testing measures are Corcoran and Fischer (1994), *Measures for Clinical Practice: A Sourcebook,* or Kane and Kane (1981), *Assessing the Elderly: A Practical Guide to Measurement.* These offer tested measurement tools that you can use to measure different variables.

However, you will not always find appropriate instruments for measuring the variables you are studying. Sometimes you may need to create your own. A survey is just an instrument that you develop to measure specific variables for your study. There are other sources of data, such as observations, interviews, or case notes.

Examples of Data Collection

In the homeless shelter study, I used four different data sources: shelter intake forms, participant observation, interviews with the shelter guests, and interviews with shelter staff. Each data source helped me understand what happens in a homeless shelter to address the problems of homeless people. One source was not sufficient, but the combination of the four sources provided a picture of what happens in a homeless shelter. For example, the intake forms had information about the reasons given by a guest for being homeless and the nature of the support systems of each guest. This was basic information and could be easily quantified or statistically measured. However, this information raised additional question about whether these reasons were actually the problems that led to being homeless or just symptoms of other problems. To verify the reasons, interviews with the shelter guests were conducted. Thus, one form of data necessitated a different type of data collection to obtain a fuller understanding of the factors leading to homelessness.

Verifying Data

Using different instruments to measure the same variable is a good way to check the reliability and validity of the data you obtain. This is one reason that surveys usually ask the same question a couple of different ways. This type of questioning can be a check and balance system to verify the validity and reliability of the data. Validity and reliability were addressed earlier when we reviewed some of the errors that can threaten a study and looked at protections against them. Therefore, you should have a variety of data sources for your study that begin to address questions of error in your data.

Data sources come from the variables in your study. How you defined your variables will dictate the different types of data and the characteristics of the data. For example, in the homeless study, I defined *homeless person* as a single adult. Therefore, my variable limited the study to only single adult homeless persons, not families nor runaway youth. This influenced the nature of the data that I collected, since I was not going to be looking at the wide range of the total homeless population but only one segment of it. In addition, other characteristics of the population were identified from the shelter intake forms. At each shelter, staff members would ask the person how he or she became homeless. Within the context of this question, there were a number of ways the person could respond. Such responses were loss of job, substance abuse, or a domestic dispute. Each of these would be an attribute to the variable of how a person became homeless.

Building on Data

Each variable has one or more attributes. For example, shelter intake forms identify a number of reasons (attributes) the person could give for being homeless. These are presented in a checklist on the intake form to help staff complete the intake process. The list includes loss of job, substance abuse, and domestic dispute. In this one variable, reason for being homeless, there were about eight different attributes. The attributes provide some parameters for structuring the data.

A problem developed when the variables with their attributes could not demonstrate whether the reason given was a cause or an effect of a larger issue that led to being homeless. Therefore, multiple data sources seeking the same information were used to gain a broader understanding of the reason someone was homeless. For one guest, Sam, substance abuse was the reason the shelter listed for his homelessness, yet the interview revealed the possibility that substance abuse was really the effect of earlier child abuse. The shelter-developed intake form was good for identifying superficial reasons for homelessness but did not identify deeper causal factors. The interview became a data source to identify possible causal factors for Sam's homelessness. The data gathered from the interview could then be used to explore how generalizable this incident was in other homeless persons. The interview identified new information relating to causes of homelessness. This new information then could be checked out to see how generalizable that situation was to other people's reasons for being homeless.

The next two pages provide a format for listing your variables, data sources, and their attributes. At times you may use preexisting tests or intake forms; at others, you will design your own source, such as a semistructured interview schedule. Whatever you choose, it is important to identify the attributes of the variable and your data source. Realize that sometimes you will identify one variable but gather data about it from different sources, as with the variable "reasons for being homeless."

Instruments and Data Sources

State your hypothesis.

The reasons that a person becomes homeless are more complex than just
a loss of social supports and require in-depth exploration (leading to an
exploratory study).

Identify your variable, how you plan to gather the information about the variable (data source), and the attributes of the variable within those data sources. Continue on a separate page if necessary.

Variable	Data Source	Attributes
Reason left last address	Intake form	Eviction; family problem; jail release; substance abuse; no money; transition to a move
Reason for needing the shelter	Intake form	Nowhere else to go; evicted; no money/income; referred
History of problem	Intake form	None; alcohol or drugs; alcohol and drugs; mental illness; alcohol, drugs, and mental illness
Contact with social services	Intake form	Probation officer; entitlement program; mental health; substance abuse; rehab

For items listed above that do not have readily available instruments, identify the characteristics (for example, the type of instrument and how it will be administered) of the instrument you plan to use. For example, if you plan to use a semistructured interview, list the questions you want covered.

Instruments and Data Sources
(continued)

Proposed Instruments	Critical Characteristics
Semistructured interviews with shelter guests	Reasons for being homeless—the following questions: "Why did you come to the shelter?" "What do you know about the social service system?" "What kind of relationship do you have with family or friends?"
Semistructured interviews with shelter staff	Reasons for being homeless—the following questions: "What do you think the problem is that brought people to the shelter?" "What can you do to help the guests in the shelter?" "What services can you provide to help the guests?"

Instrument Reliability and Validity

For each instrument selected or proposed in the previous two sections, how reliable and valid are these instruments? Continue on a separate page if necessary.

Reliability: How closely do repeated observations (by different people, at different times, etc.) of the same thing agree with each other?

Validity: With what assurance do we know that the instrument is measuring what we believe it is measuring?

Instrument	Reliability	Validity
Intake forms	To extent of getting reimbursed from state	To extent required by state
Semistructured interviews	To extent of researcher reliability	To extent of researcher validity

Instruments and Data Sources

State your hypothesis.

_____

_____

_____

_____

Identify your variable, how you plan to gather the information about the variable (data source), and the attributes of the variable within those data sources. Continue on a separate page if necessary.

Variable	Data Source	Attributes

For items listed above that do not have readily available instruments, identify the characteristics (for example, the type of instrument and how it will be administered) of the instrument you plan to use. For example, if you plan to use a semi-structured interview, list the questions you want covered.

Instruments and Data Sources
(continued)

Proposed Instruments   **Critical Characteristics**

_____   _____
_____   _____
_____   _____
_____   _____
_____   _____
_____   _____
_____   _____
_____   _____
_____   _____
_____   _____
_____   _____
_____   _____

Instrument Reliability and Validity

For each instrument selected or proposed in the previous two sections, how reliable and valid are these instruments? Continue on a separate page if necessary.

Reliability: How closely do repeated observations (by different people, at different times, etc.) of the same thing agree with each other?

Validity: With what assurance do we know that the instrument is measuring what we believe it is measuring?

Instrument   **Reliability**   **Validity**

_____   _____   _____
_____   _____   _____
_____   _____   _____
_____   _____   _____
_____   _____   _____
_____   _____   _____

▼▼▼

CHAPTER TWELVE

Data Collection Forms

I t is one thing to have instruments for data, but it is another to understand how you are going to organize your data once you have collected it. The organization of data is crucial if you are to make sense out of the information you have collected.

Different Organization for Different Data

Some data are easy to organize—for example, surveys are designed to answer particular questions. Therefore, the data on closed questions can be quantified and entered into a statistical computer program. In this treatment, certain values are assigned to delineate various aspects or characteristics of the variable. As mentioned earlier, the intake form provided the staff with a menu of reasons for people's homelessness. Each item on the menu would be assigned a numerical value to be entered into the computer. The computer can read the numbers, but you will need a code book to help you interpret the numbers.

Other data are harder to organize. For example, interviews need to be read and reread to determine whether specific themes emerge. If one appears, you must decide whether that theme relates to a variable in your study.

Ways to Organize Data

As the researcher, you make decisions on how to organize the interview data to answer the questions in your study. This may entail taking pieces of the interview and seeing how they relate to the study questions. This process is called the cut-and-paste method of qualitative research, but now there are some computer programs (NUD*IST, HyperResearch, or Ethnograph) that can assist in this process. These programs are only tools and will not replace the analysis being done by you, the researcher, in deciding whether the information fits.

Example of Data Organization

In the shelter study, my need to understand the data led to my developing a semistructured interview schedule. Five open-ended questions were used to structure the interview sufficiently so that I would get the information I needed to complete the study. As I said earlier, I would never have been able to identify a possible precipitating factor that led to Sam's becoming homeless if I had not explored deeper issues of his life. The semistructured interviews provided qualitative data that permitted me to uncover issues not readily available from the intake form. The nature of the tool you use to collect your data is very important in helping you organize the information to answer your questions. In the case of a semistructured interview, the questions act as parameters for organizing the conversation that follows. Then the researcher is responsible for identifying commonalities among subjects based upon how they answered the questions. On the following pages, indicate how you will record or organize the data for your study.

Data Collection Forms

State your hypothesis.

The reasons that a person becomes homeless are more complex than just a loss of social supports and require in-depth exploration (leading to an exploratory study).

Use the space below to sketch the forms you will use to record the data from your study. Alternatively, you may list and describe the forms below and then attach specimens. For example, if you are using a survey, attach a copy of the survey. If you plan to use an interview, attach a copy of the interview schedule you plan to use. With a survey or even an intake form that is measurable, it is helpful to create a codebook, and a partially completed coded data sheet. For example, a codebook would identify the following:

From Intake Forms (selected from codebook)

Reason left last address	1 = evicted
	2 = family problems
	3 = jail release
	4 = no money
	5 = substance abuse
	6 = move/in transit
	9 = missing

Reason for needing shelter	1 = nowhere else to go
	2 = evicted from residence
	3 = no money/income
	4 = referred by individual or social services
	9 = missing

Data Collection Forms
(continued)

This information would be organized in a chart that would look like this:

Category	Total population (%)	Shelter 1 (%)	Shelter 2 (%)
Reason left last address	n	n	n
Eviction	n	n	n
Family problem	n	n	n
Jail release	n	n	n
No money	n	n	n
Substance abuse	n	n	n
Move/in transit	n	n	n

(n is the number of cases for each category
followed by the percent of the total).

Data Collection Forms

State your hypothesis.

_____

_____

_____

_____

Use the space below to sketch the forms you will use to record the data from your study. Alternatively, you may list and describe the forms below and then attach specimens. For example, if you are using a survey, attach a copy of the survey. If you plan to use an interview, attach a copy of the interview schedule you plan to use. With a survey or even an intake form that is measurable, it is helpful to create a codebook, and a partially completed coded data sheet. For example, a codebook would identify the following:

_____

_____

_____

_____

_____

_____

_____

_____

_____

_____

_____

_____

_____

_____

_____

_____

_____

_____

_____

_____

▼▼▼
Data Collection Forms
(continued)

This information would be organized in a chart that would look like this:

_____

_____

_____

_____

_____

_____

_____

_____

_____

_____

_____

_____

_____

_____

_____

_____

_____

_____

_____

_____

_____

_____

_____

_____

_____

_____

_____

_____

▼▼▼

CHAPTER THIRTEEN

Data Analysis and Statistical Procedures

Y ou have collected your data. Now you need to decide how to analyze it.

Types of Statistics

There are descriptive statistics that summarize the variable characteristics of your sample. There are also inferential statistics that help to determine whether an observed relationship is due to chance or is a reflection of the interaction between the variables being studied. Based on the word *infer*, inferential statistics are used to generalize the results to the wider population. There are special statistical calculations that are used to provide numbers for each. For example, frequencies, means, medians, standard deviations, and so on, are all descriptive statistics that define characteristics of the data for each individual variable. Regressions, correlations, *t*-tests, chi-squares, and analysis of variance (ANOVA), are all inferential statistical procedures for examining relationship between and among variables.

Sometimes the organization is by category for data that are nominal (named), ordinal (in rank order), interval (ordered but with equal distance between properties being measured), or ratio (ordered and equidistant with the addition of a zero point). It is important to understand the type of data you are using because some tests will work with only some types of data. For example, you cannot perform a *t*-test with two variables that are both nominal; at least one has to be interval or ratio. However, you can use a chi-square test with two nominal variables.

None of the statistical tests currently measure qualitative data as it is. Qualitative data first needs to be quantified to be subjected to statistical measures. Some research computer packages will quantify your interpretation of the qualitative data to prepare it for statistical measurement.

To Test or Not to Test

I mention this because it is important to understand the value of statistical tests. Not everything is ready or can be subjected to statistical testing. It is important for you as a researcher to decide whether you want to subject your data to statistical testing. The following chart lists types of variables and appropriate tests for them.

Test	Dependent Variable	Independent Variable
Frequency	All variable types	
Mean	Interval/ratio	
Median	Interval/ratio	
Mode	Interval/ratio	
t-test*	Interval/ratio	Nominal (2 categories)
Chi-square test	Nominal or ordinal (2 or more categories)	Nominal or ordinal (2 or more categories)
ANOVA*	Interval/ratio	Nominal or ordinal (3 or more categories)
Regression	Nominal or ordinal (3 or more categories)	Nominal or ordinal (3 or more categories)

*ANOVA (analysis of variance) produces the same type of results as performing multiple t-tests. However, one cannot perform multiple t-tests, so ANOVA was created.

Source: Adapted from Statistics for Social Workers (3rd ed.) by Robert Weinbach and Richard Grinnel, 1995, White Plains, NY, Longman Publishers.

On the next page, identify your variables, the type of variable each one is, and the statistic you would perform on that variable. Then look at relationships between variables and the type of statistical test you will perform on them. If there is a group of variables that you want to test, describe the relationship and type of test you will perform.

Data Analysis and Statistical Procedures

Your plans will depend on the purpose of your research. If you are only describing your sample, descriptive statistics are useful.

State your hypothesis.

The reasons that a person becomes homeless are more complex than just a loss of social supports and require in-depth exploration (leading to an exploratory study).

Variable Name	Type of Variable	Statistic
Reason left last address	Nominal	Frequency
Reason for shelter	Nominal	Frequency
History of problem	Nominal	Frequency
Contact with social services	Nominal	Frequency
Previous days in shelter	Ratio	Mean

If you are testing hypotheses, you will want to examine the relationships among variables of the differences between groups.

Variables Examined	Relationship Examined	Statistic
History of problem and reason for shelter	Compare two types of nominal data	Chi-square
Previous days in shelter and history of problem	Compare ratio data to nominal data	ANOVA

Data Analysis and Statistical Procedures

(continued)

Groups (Combining Variables to Create a Group) to Be Compared and Variables on Which They Will Be Compared	Relationship Examined	Statistic
(History of problem and work history) in relation to previous days in shelter	Compare two sources of nominal data and compare with ratio data	ANOVA

Data Analysis and Statistical Procedures

Your plans will depend on the purpose of your research. If you are only describing your sample, descriptive statistics are useful.

State your hypothesis.

_____

_____

_____

_____

Variable Name	Type of Variable	Statistic
_____	_____	_____
_____	_____	_____
_____	_____	_____
_____	_____	_____
_____	_____	_____
_____	_____	_____
_____	_____	_____
_____	_____	_____
_____	_____	_____

If you are testing hypotheses, you will want to examine the relationships among variables of the differences between groups.

Variables Examined	Relationship Examined	Statistic
_____	_____	_____
_____	_____	_____
_____	_____	_____
_____	_____	_____
_____	_____	_____
_____	_____	_____

Data Analysis and
Statistical Procedures
(continued)

Groups (Combining Variables to Create a Group) to Be Compared and Variables on Which They Will Be Compared	Relationship Examined	Statistic
_____	_____	_____
_____	_____	_____
_____	_____	_____
_____	_____	_____
_____	_____	_____
_____	_____	_____
_____	_____	_____
_____	_____	_____
_____	_____	_____
_____	_____	_____
_____	_____	_____
_____	_____	_____

CHAPTER FOURTEEN

Protection of Human Participants

As social scientists, we are very concerned about the rights of human participants, especially around the issue of self-determination. A research project should not in any way harm the people who are involved in the study. The goal is to build knowledge, and in a human services field, the best way to build knowledge is from the people who are served.

Informed Consent

To protect the people being studied, a research proposal will contain a section safeguarding those participating in the study. Some universities use an internal review board (IRB) to dictate how you need to protect human participants. Other universities do not have IRBs. Regardless, all researchers must be committed to guaranteeing the rights of human participants. Participants in a study must be told what the study will investigate, how the results will be used, and assured that they will in no way be directly identified in the discussion of the study findings. They must also agree, generally by signing a consent form, to participate under the terms explained by the researcher. This procedure is called obtaining *informed consent* from the participants.

Example of Consent

When I conducted the homeless shelter study, I had two different consent forms: one to permit me to look at case records and a second to allow me to use the information from the interview. The second consent form stated that I would use the guest's story but would change his name to maintain his anonymity. Before I interviewed any person or looked at his or her records, each guest signed the consent form. If one did not sign the form, I was not permitted to include that person in the study.

The questions on the next two pages are standard questions that will help you develop a consent form to use with your study. If you are doing survey research, a cover letter stating the purpose of the study can suffice for a consent form. It will hold all the information you want the participants to know to protect them and their anonymity. Such reassurance will enhance their completion of the survey, so take a few minutes, review the questions, and develop your own consent form to protect the people you will be studying as well as yourself, and have each participant sign a consent form.

▼▼▼
Protection of
Human Participants

State your hypothesis.

_____

_____

_____

_____

Whenever humans are research participants, the researcher must consider the following:

A. Describe the potential risks and/or benefits of participating in the study.

_____

_____

_____

_____

_____

B. Describe the participants and their ability to consent to participate in the research (be particularly aware to protect against coercion).

_____

_____

_____

_____

_____

C. How will the participants be fully informed about the research (including its purposes and risks)? How will you assure that they have freely consented to participate?

_____

_____

_____

_____

_____

▼▼▼
Protection of
Human Participants
(continued)

D. How will you protect the confidentiality of research data?

_____

_____

_____

_____

E. Write a consent form or cover letter that includes the following elements.

Basic Elements of Informed Consent

1. Statement regarding the purpose of the research, expected duration of the individual's participation, procedures that participants are to follow, and identification of experimental procedures.

2. Description of any foreseeable risks or discomfort to participants.

3. Description of any benefits to participant or to others that would reasonably be expected.

4. Disclosure of appropriate procedures or treatments.

5. Statement describing how you will maintain confidentiality of the participants and data.

6. If the research involves more than minimal risk, provide an explanation and type of compensation to be provided if injury occurs.

7. Name of person to contact for answers to relevant questions about research.

8. Statement that participation is voluntary; refusal or withdrawal will result in no penalty or loss of entitled benefits.

9. Agreement for participation, with a signature/date line: "I have read this statement and agree to participate in the study."

▼▼▼

CHAPTER FIFTEEN

Reporting Results

It is one thing to do a study and gain knowledge. However, nothing happens to the information that you have gained unless you share it with others.

Report Your Results

There is a proverbial question about a tree: If it falls in the woods and no one hears it, does it make a sound when it falls? Similar to the falling tree, if you do a study and do not report the results, no one hears your results; no one gains from the information you acquired. Therefore, it is important to report the results of your study, regardless of whether you find new information.

Select Your
Reporting Methods

The next decision about reporting your results is how you are going to report them. There should be some logical process to how you present your findings. Realize that people learn in different ways. Some people learn better from tables, whereas others learn from graphs.

Value of Graphics

I usually find that multiple forms of data presentation are very useful. Results need to be explained, but if the explanation is combined with a table or graph, there is a visualization of what you are stating. Many times that visualization will enhance the explanation and provide clarity.

When I did the homeless shelter study, I categorized the reasons people gave for being homeless. This information appeared in table form, drawn from the data on the intake forms from the two shelters. One table was a demographic table comparing the guests at each of the shelters. The second table compared the reasons the guests gave for needing to come to the shelter. The third table identified and compared potential outside supports for the guests at each of the shelters. Explanations of the meaning of the data in these tables appeared in the text of the study but that explanation was enhanced by the tables themselves. The tables provided pictorial comparisons of the two shelters. Therefore, tables, charts, graphs, and whatever picture you can provide will enhance any information you report.

Format for Journal Articles

A brief word about writing the results of your study: At this time, you may be doing your study and writing the results only to satisfy a course requirement. Even so, our level of knowledge can always be improved; therefore, think about submitting your findings to a journal. The basic format of a journal article is as follows (Huck, Cormier, & Bounds, 1996):

1. Abstract
2. Introduction
    a. Review of the literature
    b. Statement of purpose of the study
3. Method
    a. Participants
    b. Materials
    c. Dependent variables
    d. Procedure
4. Results
5. Discussion
6. References

Complete the following pages by thinking about how you will report the results of your data.

Reporting Results

State your hypothesis.

The reasons that a person becomes homeless are more complex than just
a loss of social supports and require in-depth exploration (leading to an
exploratory study).

In the space below, sketch summary data tables and/or graphs that will reflect your results. You may use multiple tables and graphs; make sure that you include your dependent and independent variables. If it is helpful, you may include simulated results of the kind you hope to find.

The data will be presented in the following tables:

Table 2 Reasons Guests Need Shelter			
Category	Total population (%)	Shelter 1 (%)	Shelter 2 (%)
Reason left last address	n	n	n
Eviction	n	n	n
Family problem	n	n	n
Jail release	n	n	n
No money	n	n	n
Substance abuse	n	n	n
Move/in transit	n	n	n
Reason for shelter	n	n	n
Nowhere else to go	n	n	n
Evicted	n	n	n
No money/income	n	n	n
Referred	n	n	n

(continued)

Reporting Results
(continued)

Category	Total population (%)	Shelter 1 (%)	Shelter 2 (%)
History of problem	n	n	n
None	n	n	n
Alcohol or drugs	n	n	n
Alcohol and drugs	n	n	n
Mental illness	n	n	n
Alcohol, drugs, and mental illness	n	n	n
Work history	n	n	n
Regular	n	n	n
Some part-time	n	n	n
None	n	n	n

(n is the number of cases for each category
followed by the percent of the total).

Reporting Results

State your hypothesis.

_____

_____

_____

_____

In the space below, sketch summary data tables and/or graphs that will reflect your results. You may use multiple tables and graphs; make sure that you include your dependent and independent variables. If it is helpful, you may include simulated results of the kind you hope to find.

_____

_____

_____

_____

_____

_____

_____

_____

_____

_____

_____

_____

_____

_____

_____

_____

_____

_____

_____

_____

▼▼▼
Reporting Results
(continued)

▼▼▼

CHAPTER SIXTEEN

Administrative Arrangements/Agreements

We live in a society where we all need to be accountable for our own actions. It is what I call "CYB" (cover your back) and is an important rule I live by. The same is true in conducting a research project. It is important to have all the administrative details in order. These include making sure you have the resources you need to conduct the study before you begin. You need a budget that is realistic. You also must make sure that you have the resources available to conduct the study as you described it. Remember back to the sampling section: The size of the sample will be dependent on your resources.

Types of Arrangements to Be Made

I defined these concerns in the homeless shelter study. According to Glaser and Straus (1967), a person should continue doing qualitative data collection until data saturation. I was not sure when data saturation would be achieved, and because I was the only person collecting data, I had to set limits on the size of the sample that I could interview. The number I selected was realistic given the resources I had at hand. Even this would not have been possible if I had not made administrative arrangements that established parameters for the study to make it manageable and doable.

In addition, before I could conduct the study, I had to get permission from the two shelter directors to use their shelters as sites for the study. It was not sufficient to have the consent of the regional homeless commission; I had to approach each director personally and explain the purpose of the study, including a description of my role in collecting data and how it would affect the guests at the shelter. This is an important component, as neither director wanted any problems to develop as a result of my conducting the study. Both shelters were operating fine without me coming in to conduct the study. The directors wondered how things would change when I began the study. I had to be able to present the study methodology in a form that let the directors feel comfortable that I would not create any disruptions. They even wanted to approve the consent forms that I would use prior to collecting the data. The point of my telling you this is that the more information you can provide, the better will be your chance of gaining access to the population you want to study.

Planning Your Study Administration

Take a few minutes and outline the administrative arrangements for your study. Once you have completed the arrangements, think about who needs to be approached to give you the appropriate access you need to perform your study. With whom do you need a collaborative agreement to enhance the study? The key word in most funding sources these days is collaboration. The more partners you involve in the process, the better will be your chances of having the research funded. Take a few minutes and identify the people with whom you need written agreements to carry out your study.

Administrative Arrangements

State your hypothesis.

_____

_____

_____

_____

The most elegantly designed studies have sometimes collapsed for lack of attention to administrative details. Describe administrative arrangements such as project management, budget, equipment needs, supplies needed, space needed, printing, consultation, postage, telephone, computer programming, etc.

_____

_____

_____

_____

_____

_____

_____

_____

_____

_____

_____

_____

_____

_____

_____

_____

_____

_____

_____

Administrative Arrangements
(continued)

Without access to the sample or data you intend to use in the design, the study cannot be conducted. Do you need any special agreements to conduct your study? From whom do you need permission to approach your sample? Whom do you need to contact and how do you intend to do this? Discuss these issues and describe the contents of any written agreements that you need. Attach copies of any letters you need to write to obtain your data. If a mail questionnaire is to be used, write the accompanying cover letter that will be attached. If you are to use a telephone survey or interview, write a prepared speech that the interviewers will use when approaching the subject. If you need letters to administrators of social agencies, include these.

▼▼▼

CHAPTER SEVENTEEN

Limitations of the Study

Your study was designed to satisfy your interest in the topic. The goal was to answer your questions. By answering your questions, you have been able to contribute new information about your topic to the field. That is why it is important to share your findings with others.

Identifying Study Limitations

Regardless of how significant your findings are, there will be people who question them. That is all right; you should not take it as a personal attack but just the normal skepticism of people trying to find and understand truth. To counter the skeptics, identify some of the limitations of the study and share them. This action demonstrates your rational ability to think about your study and its findings critically and to share those critical thoughts with others. Knowing the limitations is also helpful for people who may want to replicate your study, thus building on the work that you have already begun. When you identify the limitations to the study, others can address them ahead of time in future research.

Examples of Limitations

I have already identified a number of limitations in the homeless shelter study. Some of these included my inability to interview non-English-speaking guests, my limiting the sample to shelters serving single adults, and the limits set on sample size. Those were limitations I knew of prior to beginning the study. During the study I found a difference between the two shelter types, as one provided home services and the other house services; this was a significant finding. The house/home issue relates to the question of generalizability. It was thought that both shelters were the same. From the data collection, it became evident that the two shelters were different in the way they provided services. This meant that the two shelters were not the same as initially expected. It was important to identify these limitations so others who want to replicate this study can address them in the planning stage

In addition, identifying limitations is a way of being honest to yourself. It is impossible to be all things to all people. Identifying the study's limitations brings a humanness to the project. It reduces criticism from others about your study because you have been self-critical. There are imperfections in everything we do; that is the nature of life. Identifying the limitations is your way of making your study realistic.

Take a few minutes to identify the limitations of your study. This can be accomplished by answering the questions on the following pages.

Limitations of the Study

State your hypothesis.

_____

_____

_____

_____

After struggling to achieve a design that is feasible and provides control of the most troublesome sources of bias, you may be left with inadequate controls over other sources of bias. Use the space below to identify these.

Potential Sources of Bias Remaining

_____

_____

_____

_____

_____

_____

_____

_____

_____

_____

_____

_____

_____

_____

_____

_____

_____

_____

_____

_____

Limitations of the Study
(continued)

Even unbiased studies have limitations in their generalizability. To what kinds of people beyond your study sample can you justify generalizing your conclusions? (It may be easier to identify individuals for whom your conclusions do not necessarily apply.)

Limitations to Generalizability

_____

_____

_____

_____

_____

_____

_____

_____

_____

_____

_____

_____

_____

_____

_____

_____

_____

_____

_____

_____

_____

_____

CHAPTER EIGHTEEN

Conclusion

You have now completed the steps in conducting a research project. Regardless of whether your study is qualitative or quantitative, the steps are similar. One type may emphasize certain areas over others—for example, quantitative research findings are more amenable to statistical analysis than qualitative findings. Qualitative research relies on you to develop different mechanisms for organizing and analyzing data; however, the essence of the steps for the two types are the same. This tool kit was designed to take the mystery out of the research process by breaking research into manageable parts. Once you have completed the steps outlined here, you need to share the knowledge you have gained with your colleagues. Refer to the section on reporting results for an outline of how research articles appear in most journals.

Remember that research is part of everything you do in your work. Even when working with client systems of all sizes, whenever you begin an assessment you are adding the data to your data banks to see whether that information is generalizable to other situations you have been exposed to. Research is only a concept used to define how we organize and analyze information. So have a good time and enjoy your research.

Bibliography

Agresti, A., & Finlay, B. (1986). *Statistical methods for the social sciences.* San Francisco: Dellen.

Allen-Meagres, P., and Lane, B. A. (1990). Social work practice: Integrating qualitative and quantitative data collection techniques. *Social Work, 35*(5), 452–458.

Anastas, J. W., & MacDonald, M. L. (1994). *Research design for social work and the human services.* New York: Lexington Books.

Arkava, M. I., & Lane, T. A. (1983). *Beginning social work research.* Boston: Allyn & Bacon.

Babbie, E. (1995). *The practice of social research* (7th ed.). Belmont, CA: Wadsworth.

Barlow, D. H., & Hersen, M. (1984). *Single case experimental design strategies for studying behavior change* (2nd ed.). New York: Pergamon Press.

Berg, B. L. (1995). *Qualitative research methods for the social sciences* (2nd ed.). Boston: Allyn & Bacon.

Berger, P. L., & Luckman, T. (1966). *The social construction of reality.* New York: Anchor Books.

Bloom M., Fischer, J., & Orme, J. (1995). *Evaluating practice: Guidelines for the accountable professional* (2nd ed.). Boston: Allyn & Bacon.

Blythe, B. J., & Briar, S. (1985). Developing empirically-based models of practice. *Social Work, 30,* 483–488.

Bronson, D. E., & Blythe, B. J. (1987). Computer support for single case evaluation of practice. *Social Work Research and Abstracts, 24*(2), 21–22.

Cook, T. D., & Campbell, D. T. (1979). *Quasi-experimentation design and analysis issues for field settings.* Boston: Houghton Mifflin.

Corcoran, K. (Ed.). (1992). *Structuring change.* Chicago: Lyceum Books.

Corcoran, K., & Fischer, J. (1994). *Measures for clinical practice: A sourcebook* (2nd ed.). New York: Free Press.

Craft, J. L. (1985). *Statistics and data analysis for social workers.* Itasca, IL: F. E. Peacock.

Donovan, R., Jaffe, N., & Pirie, V. M. (1987). Unemployment among low-income women: An exploratory study. *Social Work, 32*(4), 301–305.

Fischer, J. (1983). Evaluations of social work effectiveness: Is positive evidence always good evidence? *Social Work, 28,* 74–77.

Friedman, B. D. (1994). *No place like home.* Ann Arbor, MI: University Microfilms International.

Friedman, B. D., & Levine-Holdowsky, M. (1997). Overcoming barriers to homeless delivery services: A community response. *Journal of Social Distress and the Homeless, 6*(1), 13–28.

Glaser, B. G., & Strauss, A. L. (1967). *The discovery of grounded theory: Strategies for qualitative research.* New York: Aldine.

Grinnel, R. M., Jr., & Williams, M. (1990). *Research in social work: A primer.* Itasca, IL: F. E. Peacock.

Hammersley, M., & Atkinson, P. (1983). *Ethnography: Principles in practice.* London: Tavistock.

Hoover, K. R. (1988). *The elements of social scientific thinking.* New York: St. Martin's Press.

Huck, S. W., Cormier, W. H., & Bounds, W. G. (1996). *Reading statistics and research* (2nd ed.). New York: HarperCollins.

Kagle, J. D. (1985). *Social work records.* Belmont, CA: Wadsworth.

Kagle, J. D., & Cowger, C. D. (1984, July–August). Blaming the client: Implicit agenda in practice research? *Social Work,* pp. 347–351.

Kane, R. A., & Kane, R. L. (1981). *Assessing the elderly: A practical guide to measurement.* Lexington, MA: Lexington Books.

Klieger, D. M. (1984). *Computer usage for social scientists.* Boston: Allyn & Bacon.

Kraemer, H. C., & Thieman, S. (1987). *How many subjects?* Newbury Park, CA: Sage.

Kurtz, N. R. (1983). *Introduction to social statistics.* New York: McGraw-Hill.

Marlow, C. (1993). *Research methods for generalist social work.* Pacific Grove, CA: Brooks/Cole.

Nurius, P. S., & Hudson, W. W. (1993). *Human services: Practice, evaluation, and computers.* Pacific Grove, CA: Brooks/Cole.

Proctor, E. K. (1990, March). Evaluating clinical practice: Issues of purpose and design. *Social Work Research Abstracts,* pp. 32–40.

Reamer, F. G. (1989). The affordable housing crisis and social work. *Social Work, 34*(1), 5–9.

Reinharz, S. (1991). *On becoming a social scientist: From survey research and participant observation to experiential analysis.* New Brunswick, NJ: Transaction Publishers.

Royse, D. (1995). *Research methods in social work* (2nd ed.). Chicago: Nelson-Hall.

Rubin, A., & Babbie, E. (1997). *Research methods for social work* (3rd ed.). Pacific Grove, CA: Brooks/Cole.

Singleton, R. A., Jr., Straits, B. C., & Straits, M. M. (1993). *Approaches to social research* (2nd ed.). New York: Oxford University Press.

Sommer, B., & Sommer, R. (1991). *A practical guide to behavioral research* (3rd ed.). New York: Oxford University Press.

Strauss, A. L. (1987). *Qualitative analysis for social scientists.* New York: Cambridge University Press.

Tripodi, T., Fellin, P., & Meyer, H. J. (1983). *The assessment of social research* (2nd ed.). Itasca, IL: F. E. Peacock.

Warheit, G. J., Bell, R., & Schwab, J. J. (1977). *Needs assessment approaches: Concepts and methods.* Washington, DC: National Institute of Mental Health.

Webb, E. J., Campbell, D. T., Schwartz, R. D., & Sechrest, L. (1966). *Unobtrusive measures.* Chicago: Rand McNally.

Weinbach, R. W., & Grinnel, R. M. (1995). *Statistics for social workers* (3rd ed.). New York: Longman.

Weinbach, R. W., & Grinnel, R. M. (1996). *Applying research knowledge: A workbook for social work students* (2nd ed.). Boston: Allyn & Bacon.

Weinbach, R. W., & Yedgidis, B. L. (1991). *Research methods for social workers.* New York: Longman.

Wilson, S. J. (1980). *Recording guidelines for social workers.* New York: Free Press.

Yllo, K. (1988). Political and methodological debates in wife abuse research. In K. Yllo & M. Bogard, *Feminist perspectives on wife abuse.* Newbury Park, CA: Sage.

York, R. O. (1997). *Building basic competencies in social work research: An experiential approach.* Boston: Allyn & Bacon.

TO THE OWNER OF THIS BOOK:

I hope that you have found *The Research Tool Kit: Putting It All Together* useful. So that this book can be improved in a future edition, would you take the time to complete this sheet and return it? Thank you.

School and address: _____

Department: _____

Instructor's name: _____

1. What I like most about this book is: _____

_____

_____

2. What I like least about this book is: _____

_____

_____

3. My general reaction to this book is: _____

_____

4. The name of the course in which I used this book is: _____

_____

5. Were all of the chapters of the book assigned for you to read? _____

  If not, which ones weren't? _____

 6. In the space below, or on a separate sheet of paper, please write specific suggestions for improving this book and anything else you'd care to share about your experience in using the book.

_____

_____

_____

_____

_____

_____

Optional:

Your name: _____ Date: _____

May Brooks/Cole quote you, either in promotion for *The Research Tool Kit: Putting It All Together* or in future publishing ventures?

Yes: _____ No: _____

Sincerely,

Bruce D. Friedman